MARC BOLAN
BORN TO BOOGIE

CHRIS WELCH
SIMON NAPIER-BELL

EEL
PIE
PUBLISHING

© Nomis Productions Ltd. 1982.
First published in 1982 by Eel Pie Publishing Ltd,
45 Broadwick Street, London W1V 1FS
ISBN 0 906008 65 4

The photographs in this book appear by courtesy
of the following sources:-
Andre Csillag, Kevin Cummins, Robert Ellis,
EMI Records, Granada T.V., John Kingaby Associates,
Syndication International Ltd, L.F.I., The Official
Marc Bolan Fan Blub, Keith Morris, Denis O'Reagan,
Barry Plummer, Universal Pictorial Press Ltd,
Mike Putland, S.K.R., David Wainwright.
Cover Photographs
Front cover: London Features International
Back Cover: Elaine Bryant - London Features International

Picture Research, Debbie Geller

Lyrics to 'HIPPY GUMBO' and 'OBSERVATIONS'
(words and music by Marc Bolan) are reprinted
by permission of Westminster Music Limited.

The Official Marc Bolan Fan Club,
1st Floor, 14 Widcombe Parade,
Millbrook Place, Bath,
Avon BA2 4JT.

A Crunch Design
Typeset in News Gothic by Beryl Leitch
Printed and bound in Great Britain by
R.J. Acford, Industrial Estate, Chichester, Sussex.

4

On the morning of 16th September, 1977 I was on my way to work in a friend's car, and we decided to put the radio on. Much to my delight, 'Soul Of My Suit' was being played, and I said to myself, 'Well done Marc, you're back, and at last the D.J.'s are ackowledging that fact!' As the last strains of the song disappeared, my delight turned to total shock. Marc Bolan had been killed in a car crash.

It took a long time for me to fully come to grips with the irony of Marc's death. A career that spanned ten years had come to an end as a result of being in a car - the object of so many of Marc's songs - the final twist being that Marc never learnt to drive because of his fear of them.

During his seemingly brief years as a pop star, Marc Bolan released twenty four singles which entered the Top Fifty, his records spent 211 weeks in the charts, and in a recent survey he was rated 32nd in an 'all time greats' chart. Marc was also one of only *seven* recording artists in the history of the British recording charts to have a *hat-trick* of number ones. In fact, Marc had four number ones, with a number two stuck right in the middle of them, an achievement surpassed, at least up until the time of his death, only by Elvis Presley, the Beatles and the Rolling Stones.

Marc was an incredible character, who never forgot his fans. Where possible he would talk to you for ages - he was most certainly always aware of the need to communicate. His concerts were a delight, and even the most cynical onlooker at a Marc Bolan/T.Rex concert was left at the end knowing that he or she had witnessed pure energy on stage. Bolan was an innovator of so many things that have since become accepted as normal practice, such as the wearing of make-up by men, and without doubt he injected showmanship into a period of pop music which had still not recovered from the loss of the Beatles. One of Marc Bolan's greatest triumphs was to bring back the pop star/fan relationship that had faded since the Beatles' heyday, and he created amazing feedback from his often awestruck audiences.

It was because I had followed Marc Bolan since 1967, bought all of his records, been at what was for me the greatest concert of all time - at Wembley Empire Pool, and met Marc so many times,hat a year after his death, along with two friends, I founded the Official Marc Bolan Fan Club. We all felt that we had to do something to pay back all the good years Marc had given to us. In 1980 the structure of the fan club changed when I was joined by my wife, and from there we gathered enough strength to release 'Sing Me A Song', the first (unreleased) Marc Bolan single to appear since 1977. The minor hit, as Simon Napier-Bell refers to it, actually proved that Marc Bolan was not forgotten, and indeed will never be overlooked again.

Simon Napier-Bell and Chris Welch have written this book with an interesting slant, analysing the rise of Marc Bolan from the quiet elf who sat cross-legged crooning mystically, to the powerful self-made electric warrior.

There are certainly a lot of questions that arise from this book. Unfortunately, the one person who could answer them with an elfish grin is no longer alive.

JOHN & SHAN BRAMLEY. JULY 1982.

There was never anyone more sure of himself, more directly to the point, than Marc Bolan. In 1966 he got hold of my home number and called me up. "I'm a singer, and I'm going to be the biggest British rockstar ever, so I need a good manager to make all the arrangements'. I told him to send a tape to the office, but he said he just happened to be near where I lived so could he drop it in? Ten minutes later he rang the bell and walked through the door with a guitar round his neck. He said, 'To tell the truth I don't have a tape, but I could sing for you right now.'

Personally, I hate that. If it's bad, how much do you listen to before you say stop? And then, by cutting someone short are you going to miss the best bit, which on tape you might have spooled on to? But I had to let him do it, because the instant he walked through the door he came across with the one thing that is most needed (but usually lacking) in all rock singers. It's what most people call star-quality, but really it's nothing more than the artist seeing himself as the essential material of his own art. He devises his own unique image and lifestyle, and projects it to everyone around him. The fact that he has chosen singing, or acting or even being a politician, as the area to work in, is irrelevant. He uses himself as a painter uses a canvas, or as a sculptor uses his lump of rock. He paints himself a little, does a bit of sculpting, decides on the right clothes, and out comes a new person. A creation. A work of art. A star.

Marc, dressed in Dickensian street-urchin clothes, was about five-foot two with a mop of black curly hair, and unlike most small people he was delighted with his size.

He played down to it. To further diminish himself he chose the biggest armchair and sat in it cross-legged. He put a capo on the neck of his guitar and said 'I don't play guitar too well, but the songs are fantastic. You're going to love them'. He wasn't boasting, or being immodest. To him the songs really were amazing and exciting. The fact that he'd found them inside himself rather than lying around lost in the street was no reason to lessen the praise he gave them. He didn't think of them as specifically his. He just happened to have come across them, and he wanted to share them with everyone.

He sang for fifty minutes and after each song he asked if I'd had enough. In the end I only stopped him to ring up and book a recording studio. We went there at once, at eight o'clock in the evening, and started the songs again from the top.

He'd invented a unique wavering voice, and coupled with his deft verbal imagery, it gave the songs an eerie quality that was perfectly matched to his elfin image. He really did know what he was doing. Afterwards, it was nearly ten and I was getting hungry, so I invited him to have dinner with me. During the starters I asked him a lot of questions, and he told me what his songs were really about, and how he'd arrived at the subjects. Also, how he'd developed his unique singing voice: he played Billy Eckstine 45s at 78 and copied the result. For the main course, he subjected me to the Marc Bolan management examination. He explained that he'd put a lot of thought into who should manage him, and he didn't want to get it wrong. He'd rejected the idea of Brian Epstein: 'too middle-class, too Jewish, too provincial; he'd want to put me in a pretty suit and make me fit for the neighbours to see'. And he'd decided against Andrew Oldham: 'He was alright when he was camping around like a little girl, but Mick Jagger's stolen all his mannerisms and Andrew's had to take up being butch. Well you know what the newly converted are like! He's running around town like a cross between Billy The Kid and Al Capone.'

Marc really amazed me. He looked about fifteen, yet he'd picked up more knowledge of the musicbusiness than seemed logically possible. Even more surprising was that while his songs were full of magical fantasy and fairy-tale imagery, he could sit down at a dinner-table and make ruthlessly down-to-earth judgements on other people.

As we started on the dessert he asked me, 'What about sex? What are you into?' I told him, 'My sex-life has an individuality all of its own.' And I wondered why I was putting up with all this. Perhaps I was interested to see if he'd give me a pass-mark, and invite me to become an honorary member of his fanclub. He told me, 'Most people talk about sex as physical attraction, but I think it's all mental. for instance when I kiss someone that isn't physical. I'm after their minds. It's what's inside their head I'm trying to get at.' I thought, 'My God, he's the elfin-vampire, feeding on the intellect of his victims. That's why he's so damned clever.' He said, 'I think I'd like to come back and spend the night with you.' This was getting uncomfortable. 'I don't think that's a good idea. You might suck my brain out and steal it.' 'But once I've had a look at it, I promise to put it back'. 'Plus twenty per cent of yours', I reminded him. 'If you want a manager you're going to have to pay for it.'

The next day I went back to the studio and listened to the tapes we'd made the night before. On second listening the songs seemed even better. It was the intensity of the singing, the shrewd imagery of the words. His performances were so gripping that I felt sure they'd get

through to anyone, provided they bothered to listen. So I called up Marc and said, 'Yes, OK, I'll manage you. Come on over and we'll start making plans.' He wasn't overawed by my acceptance. When he arrived he shrugged coolly and said, 'I knew you were going to say yes. It's the songs, isn't it? They're so nice, aren't they, man?' This off-handed immodesty should have been his most annoying quality. But really, it was the most delightful thing about him. It wasn't boastful, it was genuine appreciation of the creative qualities he found inside himself. And everything he said in praise of these qualities was accompanied by the most magnetically attractive smile; open and genuine, never turned on for effect.

I had a copy of the tape we'd recorded, so I played it and we listened. There was one song in particular that had a superb haunting quality, with eerie ear-catching couplets. "Met a man, he was nice, said his name was Paradise. Didn't realise at the time that his face and mind were mine. Hippy Gumbo, he's no good, chop him up for firewood. Hippy Gumbo, he's no good; chop him up and burn the wood." I told him: 'That's the one. If you record that and get it right you'll have a smash.'

He didn't agree at all.

'I wasn't thinking of making a record, man. I don't think that's cool. I thought we'd just do a big poster. A picture of me, just like I am. Put it all over London. People are crying out for someone like me. All it needs is a poster.' His ego was astounding, but it was born of naivety, and I had to try and explain the workings of the music industry to him. He was implacable. The charming smile disappeared, a petulant pout took its place, and I was confronted with a spoilt, demanding child. 'No, man! I've already made one record, for Decca. And it didn't get anywhere. It's an image I want now. A photograph.'

After only half-an-hour we'd arrived at our first management crisis. So I settled down to a detailed explanation of the public's psyche. The need for tangible evidence of Marc's musical genius to back up the poster. After ten minutes I began to get through to him, and the pout softened to a pucker, and finally to a smile as he began to conceive new possibilities for marketing the character he was creating.

He waved his hand airily, 'OK man, we'll release that tape you made, as an album.' 'But you can't' I explained. 'You're not ready to sell an album. It'll have to be a single. One of these songs has to be taken and re-arranged.' And then we were into a second argument, because he insisted the songs were perfect as they were. Just guitar and voice. A moment in Marc Bolan's life captured on tape in all its naturalness. But eventually, I got through yet again. I persuaded him the song should have a subtle instrumentation to augment his acoustic guitar; a small string section playing staccato chords. But no bass or drums. Once the idea had lodged in his mind it became very much his own.

'It's going to be real nice man,' he told me. 'Those strings are meant to be the trees, and I'm like the kid lost in the woods. People are going to hear that when they listen to it. They're going to thank me for making such a beautiful record.'

There were only five major record companies in England at that time, and I took the tape round to all of them and listened to their comments.

'I like the backing but I don't like the song.'
'I like the song but I don't like the backing.'
'Hate the voice but the ideas are great.'
'Love the voice but he doesn't seem to have any ideas.'

'It's great. A smash. But it's not quite right for us.'

Well, that's the music business. In the A & R department of a record company you never find yourself dealing with anyone very shrewd. Otherwise they'd be out there on their own, making a fortune independently. Still, they're the entry-point to all major record companies and some attention has to be paid to them, however tedious that may seem. So, instead of going back to Marc and telling him what I really thought of their comments, I gave him a lecture about the necessity of commerciality.

'Look, you're an artist. You see things your way and interpret things your way and want nothing more from life than to do just that. But an artist is an unreasonable person. He thinks society should support him for the benefit it gets from having his objective point-of-view. These people at record companies are normal, reasonable people. They see what the artist does as simply one more stage in the production of pieces of black plastic which they have to sell. It's no use thinking they're interested in your artistry or vision. They want a saleable piece of music to make their plastic marketable. And you're not giving it to them.'

Marc was deflated. He thought the world was going to love him. As I spoke to him he went deathly white and his body tensed up. His ego had been in such confident high gear. He had no defence ready for a shock like this. He said, 'OK, what do I have to do? I'll do whatever they want, whatever you tell me.' I was surprised. Where had the uncompromising artist gone? 'Don't be so silly. These people are full of shit. Just stick to what you're doing. Don't listen to them.' 'No, man, we've got to do what they say. I don't want you to blow it with all this art crap. I wanna be a star.' He was tight-lipped and frighteningly serious, and as he said the word 'star', he smashed his fist on the table. Then he ran to the toilet and I heard him vomiting.

He hid there for almost twenty minutes. When he came out he had none of his usual super-cool charm, but at least he'd recovered his artistic integrity. 'You're right. I won't change a thing. They're just an ignorant bunch of cunts.'

I eventually persuaded EMI to release 'Hippy Gumbo', not because they had any faith in it, but because I was manager of the Yardbirds, who were also on EMI. It didn't get one radio play. And at that time, at the height of pirate radio, it was very surprising that a person in my position couldn't persuade one single producer or DJ to play it at least once. Everyone was unanimous in their dislike of it. They hated Marc's high wobbly voice.

But I loved his voice, and his songs, and his lyrics, and his own personal style. And everyone else objecting to them made me all the more determined to succeed with him. We went through all the songs again, trying to find something more obviously suitable to pop single format.

His lyrics were fascinating. Sometimes funny, sometimes eerie and evocative, but always sparkling with good rhymes and interesting words. And they could tell you a lot about his love of observing people around the city, and hanging out with all sorts of different types.
"Wearin' shades 'n diggin' spades
'n shakin' it in West One.
Smoking charge, riding barges,
Cutting out, high-strung
I meet up with the guys
Who make like Barbara Streisand.
Dancin' 'stead of walkin',
Like they're the best one."

His greatest talent was to dream, and fantasy was what most of his songs were about. In fact, it was what most of his life was about. Everything he told you about himself was augmented with an enormous imagination. The smallest events became exciting, colourful stories, and even Marc himself frequently seemed to lose touch with the real person behind the fantasy he was creating.

He told me his parents were French, that he had been born in France, but he also told me stories of his childhood in the East End, of helping his Mum down the market. His Dad was a taxi driver some days and other things on others. One thing he always enjoyed telling people was that he'd been a top teenage model, travelling all over Europe modelling the latest male fashions for Italian and French couturiers.

Also, while he was in Paris he'd met a wizard who could levitate himself and make magic potions from rats' feet and lizards. Marc had lived with him for a year, learning the secrets of witchcraft. The truth was, one Friday night Marc had gone to Paris for the weekend and met a gay conjurer who'd invited him back for the night. By Monday morning Marc was back in London and all the rest was fantasy.

One day he told me he'd written a song about a girl in a Brazilian brothel. She'd been taken from a slum jungle dwelling outside Manaus and sold to a brothel-keeper in Sao Paulo. Her father had come to the city looking for her, but eventually he died in a street brawl without ever locating her. Her mother was left back in the jungle slum with the girl's three sisters and two brothers and no-one to support them. The story went on for a long time, in vivid detail, and I was looking forward to Marc playing me the song. It seemed like it would be a long one, a ballad that told the whole sad story. But when it came it was just three lines:- "Sarah Crazy Child is devouring all the street, with her pastel coloured dress and her seductive bongo beat. She's only just sixteen and she's forgotten how to dream." Like all his songs, the lyrics were vivid and to the point. But to write those few words he first had to conceive a whole story in great detail.

Marc was always totally turned on by the sound of words, so much so that he could fall in love with anyone if they had the right name. He told me about an actor friend he'd stayed with for a while called Riggs O'Hara. For Marc it was a magic name. 'Riggs' sounded tough and Texan. Oil wells and rugged clothes. 'O'Hara' was Hollywood glamour and romance. The name so stimulated his imagination that he never saw the person. His description of his friend was the most astoundingly inaccurate I'd ever heard. Not that there was anything wrong with Riggs O'Hara - he was a gentle, short, slightly roly-poly-shaped actor with a rather high-pitched voice. But Marc had seen a glamorous macho superman.

Before he'd come to see me, Marc had made a record with an American producer called Jim Economides - again, he'd been seduced by the sound of a name. Jim Economides was an expatriate American who'd come to London to try and interest the British in drag-racing. To Marc, 'Economides' had the sound of Greek legend about it. Gods on Mount Olympus, sun-bronzed soldiers, Achilles, Hermes, Spartacus. He'd expected to be carried to international fame by a music-business warrior, a Tin Pan Alexander-the-Great. But instead he got your average run-of-the-mill American hypester, trying his luck in the U.K. 'cos things weren't working out so good back home. Perhaps, even with me, it had been the name that first attracted Marc to ask me to be his manager. Anyway, it didn't matter much, because I'd now agreed. And every morning at eight o'clock Marc turned up at my flat, having taken a workmens' 'special' bus from Wimbledon where he

lived in a prefab with his Mum and Dad. He'd make me a cup of tea, climb into my bed, and discuss our plans for his future success.

He said he wanted to be a super-charged, super-dynamic, space-age rockstar. He had it clearly in his mind. Elvis and the Beatles had been mere trivia. Marc Bolan was going to be the energy centre of the Universe. A new mega-sun, perhaps God himself.

I was stuck with a more mundane problem: how to get this kid his first radio play. To give him ideas, I took him along to a Yardbird's recording session. During a blues number, Jeff Beck played a solo that consisted of one sustained note hanging lazily over the whole twelve-bar chord sequence. Marc fell in love with it. He took an acetate of the track back to my flat and lay on the floor in front of the record-player listening to Jeff's one-note solo time after time. For a week it was the biggest influence in Marc's life. Then he went back to his other old favourite: Dylan's 'Blonde On Blonde' double album.

I was managing another group called John's Children. They were outrageously bad, but devotedly energetic, and with a good guitarist-come-songwriter they might begin to get somewhere. So I tentatively suggested to Marc that he might join them. 'They've got a following already,' I explained to him. 'You'd get at least a quarter of their fans for yourself. You could do some of the singing in the group and begin to get people used to your voice. Also, you could write all the songs and be sure they're recorded the way you wanted them.' I thought he'd refuse outright, but the frustration of nothing happening was too great, and he began to lean towards the idea.

Finally, over dinner, he agreed, but he also made an amazing (in retrospect) chance remark. We were discussing his heroes. They were a strange bunch: Elvis Presley, Audie Murphy, Mighty Joe Young - but above all, James Dean. Marc loved Dean's image and the mythology that had grown out of his death. I tried to use this to my advantage in persuading him to join John's Children. I said, 'Joining the group will start you off on the path to eventual stardom. And you gotta start getting rich soon if you're going to be like James Dean and buy a Porsche.' 'Oh no,' Marc told me, 'a Porsche wouldn't be right for me. I'm too small. I think a mini is the right car for me. If I was going to die in a car crash, it ought to be a mini. I think I'd like that. It'd be nice.'

Putting Marc into John's Children had really been Kit Lambert's idea. He was the Who's manager and had also started his own record label: Track Records. His first two signings to Track were Jimi Hendrix and John's Children, but part of the deal with John's Children was that Marc would join them and play guitar. Jimi Hendrix being on Track was one of the main factors that helped persuade Marc. Hendrix was his new hero, and Marc digested every bit of Hendrix's wild masculinity, miniaturised it, and regurgitated it half-size - lacking in technique maybe, but not in vitality. It worked. And suddenly John's Children became an exciting live group.

Their first record for Track was 'Desdemona', with a held-back throbbing rhythm. Andy Ellison sung the verses and Marc joined him on the choruses. But though the sixties were meant to be swinging and liberated the BBC couldn't accept such words as 'rude' and 'nude', so the record was banned. Or perhaps it was because of the last line of the song: "Lift up your skirt and fly". The BBC may have thought this was some sort of terrible 'double entendre'. In fact it was Marc's love of Woods and Wizards coming to the surface yet again. Desdemona was meant to

fly off on her broomstick. Anyway, since the BBC didn't see it that way, the record was confined to Radio Caroline, and was only a minor hit.

But Marc was getting used to things not happening overnight, and he didn't seem too disappointed. Besides, he was getting on well with the group, happily joining in with the general image-building. He had his hair cut short and cute and put on all-white clothes to join them for a series of photo sessions. But even so, he was a distinct 'outsider', and he never really joined in the relationship wholeheartedly. At rehearsals he always brought along his girl-friend and left her sitting quietly at the back of the room. If there was a break for coffee he'd go and talk to her and leave the rest of the group to themselves. Once, the group was invited to a party. Marc was as eager as anyone else to go to it, but when they arrived, Marc found a large doll's house in an upstairs children's playroom and climbed inside. For the next three hours he sat, cooped-up but happy, watching through the tiny windows as the rest of the party carried on around him. Sometimes he'd shout out to people and ask for drinks to be brought. And then, at two in the morning when the party finished, he climbed out, happy as can be, thanked his host for a great party, and went off home with the rest of the group in their car.

John's Children managed to get a reasonably sized hit in Germany and Kit Lambert suggested they go off on tour with the Who. Together, the group and I devised an act of stunning bad taste. Andy ran round the audience half-naked, throwing feathers in the air, then came back onto the stage to fight viciously with John, the bass-player. Meanwhile, Chris, the drummer, destroyed his drum kit and anything else that got in his way. While all this went on, Marc strode angrily round the stage with a great necklace of one-inch chains, lashing wildly at anyone who came within reach. Music wasn't completely forgotten, but theatre came first, and Marc loved it. For three nights he played his part supremely well, but on the fourth night everyone went too far. We were at Ludwigshaven, and the stage was the biggest yet. So too were the bouncers, and they'd heard about our crazy act from the promoters of the previous gigs. They were determined to stop us going too far. They formed a line across the front of the stage, as much concerned to protect the audience from the group, as the group from the audience.

Chris went on stage and smashed into the drums and there was an enormous roar of anticipation from the twelve thousand-strong crowd. Then John and Marc launched into a driving riff, and Andy leapt out of the wings, carrying two pillow-cases of feathers. He shot across the stage, vaulted right over the heads of the assembled bouncers, landed in the front aisle and started running. The audience went berserk. They grabbed at him, but he dodged them. Three of the bouncers leapt off the stage to try and get him, and the entire auditorium erupted into a riot. Somehow Andy made it to the back, slinging feathers everywhere. He sprinted across the back aisle, weaved his way past a waiting pair of bouncers, and set off back to the stage, still dispensing fistfuls of ducks' fluff in all directions. It was unbelieveable that he could dodge so many people. Half were helping him get through and the other half were trying to stop him. The end result was all-out civil war amongst the audience. The feathers hung over the auditorium like a pall of smoke, and with everybody fighting, and chairs being smashed, the whole place looked like a disaster area. Back in front of the stage two bouncers barred Andy's way. But another one, confused at just what they were meant to be doing, helped him up and rock club in Covent Garden. He auditioned the musicians a few hours before the gig, choosing them either for alliteration in their names, or the 'coolness' of their image. Then he took them off to the Electric Garden, where he thought God would weld them into a highly cohesive musical force.

The appalling cacophony that emerged suggested a total lack of interest by God, and it led to an even greater lack of interest from the audience. Marc was shattered, and after the gig he came to me and told me he was never going to play an electric instrument again for the rest of his life. 'Man, I want to be safe. I just want to perform so I know it can't go wrong. Just me, no group, no electronics. Like that Indian cat we saw in Luxembourg.' It was the beginning of 'flower-power' and people were turning to natural things. Yoghurt, wholemeal bread and acoustic guitars. Marc saw a budding audience for his new ideas. He bought himself a prayer mat and a couple of joss sticks and then looked round for a good-looking boy to sit on the mat with him. Again he chose a name rather than a person - Steve Peregrine Took was offered the job of knocking on a bongo or two while Marc got on with the meat of the music.

I thought the results were interesting, if a bit fey. But I was disappointed that many of the best and sharpest songs were not included. With his new hippie image, Marc thought some of the older songs should be disowned. Sharp social observation was out. His new audience were all on acid, and Marc conjured up endless tales of Goblins and Hobbits and Faeries and Wizards for them. It was decidedly non-commercial, and it was plain that for a while Marc was going to perform for nothing more than a free joint or a lump or two of sugar. Marc sent a copy of 'Hippy Gumbo' to DJ John Peel, who had a late-night programme on Radio London called 'The Perfumed Garden'. Marc pretended the record was sent by a fan and by a great piece of good fortune John Peel listened to it and loved it. The style of the song fitted exactly with the direction of his programme, and he started to play it every night. On the strength of this progress I fixed up a recording session. We went off to the studios and Steve and Marc sat on a rug amongst incense burners and recorded nearly an hour of the new songs.

I couldn't persuade anyone at Track, or any other record company, that the songs had any commercial viability. so I thought the time had come to admit to Marc that my management couldn't guarantee his group an instant hit. I told him, 'It won't help you having a manager like me just at the moment. The sort of audience you're after are firmly anti-commercial.You'll need to adopt a totally hippie image to fit in with them. It would be positively harmful to have a pushy manager phoning up and trying to get you an extra ten pounds for each gig.' I offered him his contract back, on the basis that if he wanted me to, I'd help for nothing from behind the scenes. He agreed that he had to appear to be a part of the anti-commercial, anti-establishment, hippie movement, that having a conventional music-businessmanager would be harmful to what he was trying to achieve. He took his contract, thanked me, and walked up the road to Brian Morrison's office, where, a few hours later, he signed a new contract with another equally conventional music-business manager.

It's difficult to know how much Brian Morrison, or any of the other subsequent managers, actually helped or hindered Marc's rise to eventual superstardom. But the one person who really did help was a record-producer who fell in love with the music of Tyrannosaurus Rex. Tony Visconti helped make the early records the way Marc

walloped the other two.

Andy grabbed the mike and launched into the first song, and although the audience was already in full madness, the sound of his voice roused them even further. The place was wildly dangerous, with the thug bouncers hitting anyone they could grab hold of. Two of them got Andy by the leg and tried to pull him off the stage. Marc threw his guitar at them, grabbed his chains and slashed at the bouncers. His guitar's manic feed-back echoed through the auditorium like death screams.

Then the riot-police arrived.

They came in at the back of the hall and started to fight their way to the front through twelve thousand demented youths. I rushed on stage and yelled at the group to get off and get out. John and Andy headed for the dressing-room, but I grabbed them and pulled them through a side door. In the car park three bouncers suddenly appeared, and started chasing us as we ran towards the car. Then the fire brigade arrived. They turned the hoses on us as we leapt into my car, but somehow I got it started and out of the car park before the full force of the water hit us. I screeched through the town, found the autobahn, set the speed at a steady hundred and pointed us at the nearest border.

Andy had dislocated something in his neck and sat in agony with his head pointing sideways like a deformed parrot. Chris' face had been smashed by a bottle and he had a cut eye. Marc and John both had nose-bleeds. After a while I told them: 'I think the stage act's coming together quite well.' They didn't seem too cheered up by my comment, so I suggested that they should think of what had taken place as a triumph. After all, it's not everyone who manages to be expelled from the German rock circuit. Marc was the first to get over his bloodied nose and start to see the event as the fine bit of theatre it had been. And quite soon the others joined him.

To celebrate, we decided to drive home by a long route and turn it into a holiday. We started by going over the mountains to Luxembourg, and when we got there I saw a poster announcing that the Indian sitarist Ravi Shankar was giving a concert. I persuaded them we should all go.

Marc was transfixed. In Ludwigshaven he'd lost out on his ambition to be a miniaturised Hendrix, but here was a new image, all set up and ready to go. He left the concert glowing with ideas, and he told me, 'Man, if John's Children doesn't work out, I'm going to buy myself a rug and a joss-stick and sit on the floor like that Indian cat.'

Because of the way they left the German tour, John's Children came back to England without their equipment. After a few days I sent a roadie back to collect it, but the promoter of the tour had decided to steal it for himself. It was locked up in a club he owned. I flew over to Germany and organised a raiding party, but it was a dismal failure and the equipment ended up staying put, aggravatingly out of reach behind locked doors and endless legal complications.

This caused a slight hiatus in John's Children's activities and Marc started making a few plans for himself. He came to me and said that while he didn't want to leave the group, he'd nevertheless like to form a second group of his own. He was going to call it Tyrannosaurus Rex because it would eventually become the biggest rock group the world had ever seen, and Tyrannosaurus Rex had been the biggest monster ever to roam the earth.

I said I'd help him get the group together, but he wanted to tackle it all alone. He put an advertisement in Melody Maker asking for musicians, and he simultaneously got himself a gig at the Electric Garden, a seedier than seedy wanted to make them. Then, over three years, Tony patiently worked Marc round to having another try at straightforward commercialism. Bit by bit Marc had fallen into the trap of 'purism'. The people who became the group's fans were hippies rebelling against food preservatives and electric guitars, clean shaven faces and proper drum kits. Marc was already taking a risk by washing and shaving - to have played electric guitar would have been going too far.

But behind his easy-going smile, Marc was seething with impatience. He was imprisoned in a homogenized hippie ideal, but inside he was dying to be the Marc Bolan he'd dreamed of, the electrified rock god. But he was scared of losing what he'd built up and still not getting what he wanted - the debacle at the Electric Garden was a perpetual recurring nightmare to him, even after three years.

Eventually, with Tony Visconti's patient help, he took the plunge and reverted to a rock line-up, and he made it. And when he did...? Well! It just wasn't worth the bother of explaining all that crap to the people who said he'd sold out. Now he was God. And who'd ever heard of God selling out? Or having to explain himself?

I followed his career attentively, and if we happened to meet he was always cheerful and friendly. But he wasn't too happy when I decided to release all the tracks I'd recorded when he'd been with me. I put them out on Track records in 1971. It's difficult to know why he didn't want them released, but it seemed the reasons were commercial. By now, Marc was being marketed by his own corporation. He was a glossy, highly-polished, shrink-wrapped product. And he was in charge. He told the press about sales figures and gross receipts, he lectured the record company about distribution and marketing techniques, and he was setting up his own record label. Because of the huge amount of money he was asking them for, EMI were concerned about the amount of old material that might be put on the market to compete with his current records. The tracks I wanted to release were an obstacle to his commercial goals, and he tried to stop them going out. Track put them out anyway, but they didn't sell a lot. A few years later, Track records went broke and I took the tapes back. I wanted to finish them off the way we originally intended, adding the instrumentation that the songs cried out for. But remembering how much Marc had objected to them going out in 1971, I never bothered.

When he died I thought of it again, but I knew the critics would call it 'cashing-in' on his death, so I still didn't do it. But in 1981, when his fan club put out an old recording that became a small hit, I thought, 'Now's the time.'

I went into the studios and carefully edited all his old songs into cohesive shape, then added backing tracks to his singing and guitar playing. It took quite a while, and it involved listening to all the records he'd ever made. By the time I'd finished I'd spent nearly a month with nothing but Marc Bolan and his music in my mind. I thought to complement the album there should be a biography of Marc, something that would really give a good impression of who and what he was. So I commissioned pop writer Chris Welch to go and talk to all the people who were involved with Marc, and to try and fill in a few of the gaps in our knowledge of him. What follows is the result of Chris' research. It first appeared inside the album, 'You Scare Me To Death', on Cherry Red Records.

SIMON NAPIER-BELL.

Paris, 1982.

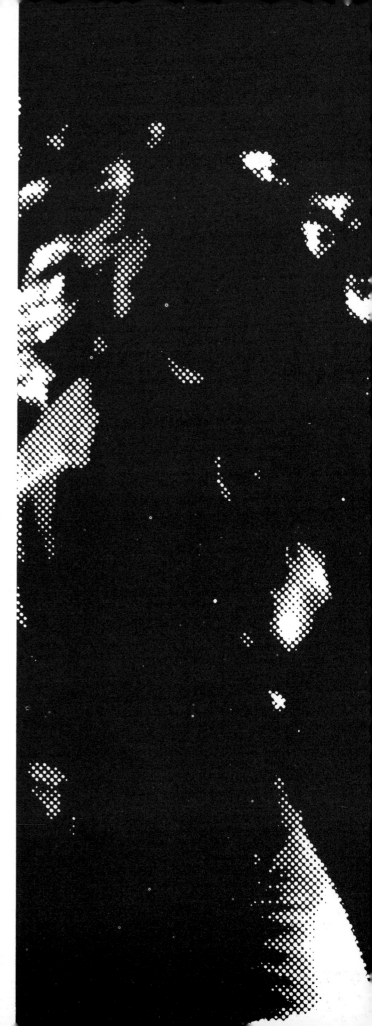

A milling mob of girls cluster around the railings outside a London townhouse, giggling, pushing, autograph books at the ready. Squeals of excitement. A white Rolls Royce glides towards them and out flounces a diminutive figure, all fur, feathers and smiles. "Good morning girls!" says the apparition with a sultry, suggestive Mae West swagger.

"Marc!" scream the fans, as photographers thrust forward with cries of "Look this way please," and "Just one more." A huge bouncer propels his charge up the steps and into the house where the star pauses dramatically to greet an old friend. He throws his arms around him in a huge, affectionate hug.

"Champagne!" demands the centre of attraction loudly. He is imperious, proffering kisses all round to the select waiting inside. If this performance causes surprise, he doesn't care. For five years he has been working, striving, and *this* is Marc Bolan's finest hour.

Marc goes into overdrive. The old friend, recovering his breath from the embrace, notices that the singer has put on weight and grown puffy. The once mild, elfin humorist has grown harsh and strident. The Bolan conversation, always so stimulating and amusing, has become an incessant stream of verbiage.

If anyone else tries to join in or merely cough, he raises his voice to drown the opposition. The flow of words is sufficient to defeat the fastest shorthand note-taker.

But the assembly forgives his outrageous swaggering and raise their glasses in a toast.

Marc is obviously enjoying himself, and there is no way to stop him, beyond having him debagged and thrown out into the street. "No, no, no — listen to me man!" gallops Bolan, as a journalist attempts a few desultory questions.

They didn't always listen to Marc, not in the early days. When you've had five top-ten hits, you can afford to tell the world to shut up and take notes. It is 1971, and the sharp-witted young man from Hackney is in the throes of stardom, that ecstatic state where artistic, popular and financial success are blended into a joyous celebration of self.

Many dream of stardom, but few are prepared for its arrival. Some become tongue-tied, irascible and confused. They take refuge in baiting the press, or erecting a wall around them. Van Morrison, Bob Dylan and Elvis Presley were all useless at handling fans.

Marc Bolan knows exactly how to cope. For a short while at least, he revels in the whole camp and theatrical spectacle. It is part of his life's work — making dreams come true. But if he were simply an egomaniac, he would be very dull indeed, and Marc is never that. He is full of the most surprising contradictions, and like all successful people he has trodden on some toes and revealed a dark side to his nature. To some he seems shrewd and manipulative. But Marc is warm, loyal, generous. The kid who got beaten up at school, who practised guitar in front of the bedroom mirror, is being hailed as the King of Glam-Rock, the Superstar of the Seventies, the teeny-bopper's delight.

He can afford a long, last laugh.

Eating strawberries and cream and drinking more champagne with the press on a hot summer's day, Marc laughs ever more loudly at other people's jokes. But he's not really listening; he's waiting for the moment when he can pour out his own creative word play. He talks in a bizarre mixture of American rock-slang, haughty well-spoken English, Cockney ribaldry and nasal hippie whine. "Hey man, that's really neat — ennit!" The eyes grow hard and black, the smile broadens into a devilish leer as he exhausts the mental capacity of lesser mortals.

Marc in the dressing room at the TV station, beams into the mirror surrounded by hot light-bulbs, adds a touch of mascara and eye liner, and regards himself with amused tolerance. Even Marc Bolan finds Marc Bolan a bit of a strain at times. Called to the set he goes into a suggestive routine as he lies on his back with his guitar over his crutch. "Ere, Marc", calls a tense voice from the control room. And the producer tells his worried assistant: "I'll have to warn him about that."

Marc, philosophical, stems the criticism from those who think their underground hero has sold out.

"I always wanted to be a rock 'n' roll star," he says between sessions on the studio floor. "But even when I was young and used to go to the TV studios, I could see Cliff Richard's pink jacket was a bit tatty, and it was a twelve-'n-six black shirt. I never lost the feeling for pop. It was always there. I went through the flowers and peace period, but I don't feel that way anymore. It's not a very peaceful period, and I don't feel that way anymore. It's not a very peaceful world. I want to boogie — but with good words as well."

The transformation of Marc Bolan from the cross-legged minstrel into strutting rocker was surprising to many. It came when many of the artists who created the 'underground' music of the Sixties spread their wings and flew. Pink Floyd, who had pioneered tacky light-shows in Covent Garden basements, now sold albums around the world. If only to survive, it was inevitable that his first band, Tyrannosaurus Rex, should reach out for wider acceptance. But when success came, it was none the less astonishing.

Back to 1971. Marc in America, trying to repeat the success of 'Ride A White Swan' and 'Hot Love' in a cold, bare rockclub in Long Island, some miles outside New York. He is supporting Humble Pie, who are surprised to find him there. Marc seems disorganized, unhappy, not at all his usual exuberant self.

The battle to win the States has just begun, and all the trade advertising in the world doesn't really help when it's just you and someone beating bongos, trying to attract the attention of a roomful of drunken louts wandering around with cans of beer waiting for Steve Marriott and Peter Frampton, the stars of the evening. This is the harsh, unglamourous face of rock 'n' roll. It begins to explain the

Bolan defence mechanisms. He suffers this indignity and cold rejection with brave stoicism. "Hi man" he says, greeting the unexpected arrival of an English rock-reporter at this inopportune moment, "When are you going back to England?" They share the flight back into London the next day and not a word is wasted on the night before, when T. Rextasy bit the dust.

Instead, Marc dances in the queue for the luggage, wearing a green bomberjacket with "Born To Boogie" stitched on the back, and prepares to inform waiting reporters in London that his American tour has been a gigantic success.

"It was sensational," he says, without a trace of shame. The hustler dances a few more deft side-steps around reality. If it didn't happen this time, then it should have done, and certainly will, next time around.

"You know, it's all fun," says Marc later. "People shouldn't take things so seriously."

In the years after his death, so sudden and tragic, a strange, mutual silence fell. A friend had gone, and eulogizing seemed pointless. But after a while his contribution, influence and achievement has begun to slip into perspective.

During his life Marc enjoyed and suffered severely fluctuating fortunes. He knew what it was like to be adored and revered, and to be abused and reviled. He was jeered at and ignored, feted and praised. His commanding, demanding presence has gone, and the shock of his death has faded, but his music has maintained a remarkable relevance. To a new generation he has become a star once more, untainted by human foible or weakness, beyond the reach of critics. Marc would have liked that.

Bolan went through three character changes during a musical career that spanned the years from 1966 to his death in 1977. His moods and personality traits overlapped and intertwined, but during the early stages, when he was attempting to establish himself, first as a solo performer and later as part of various groups, he appeared quiet, introspective, softly spoken and shy. He didn't drink or smoke, and never swore. The famous Bolan smile was fresh and casual. He seemed slightly suspicious and wary of strangers, managers and publicists. He needed help, but wasn't entirely sure if those who stepped forward were right and proper or could be trusted.

Some could recognize the seeds of stardom, but few could relate Marc's undoubted charisma to the cold statistics of singles and album sales. His music had an amateurish, homemade and ramshackled appeal; it was a long way from Tamla Motown or the Beatles, and didn't fit into the noise, smoke and psychedelic madness of the new hippies.

But Bolan's charm and perseverance worked on the media, and his music - a frail, clattering, agonized clamour - won the hearts and minds of bedsitter land with long-lost singles like 'The Wizard' to mull over, and albums like 'My People Were Fair' on the Regal Zonophone label.

Marc was the antithesis of all the vulgar, brawling blues bellowers who dominated the scene, a welcome antidote to the guitar and drum thunder-machine. He was an artist who tantalized with his apparent dedication to a mysterious cause.

In all his interviews and conversations at that time Marc talked with touching sincerity about elves, gremlins, magic, mystical beasts, gods and birdlings suckled on the tongues of the Wise One. Bolan was a poet, dedicated to the woods of knowledge. If his rhymes proved somewhat baffling on close inspection, at least he created the *effect*

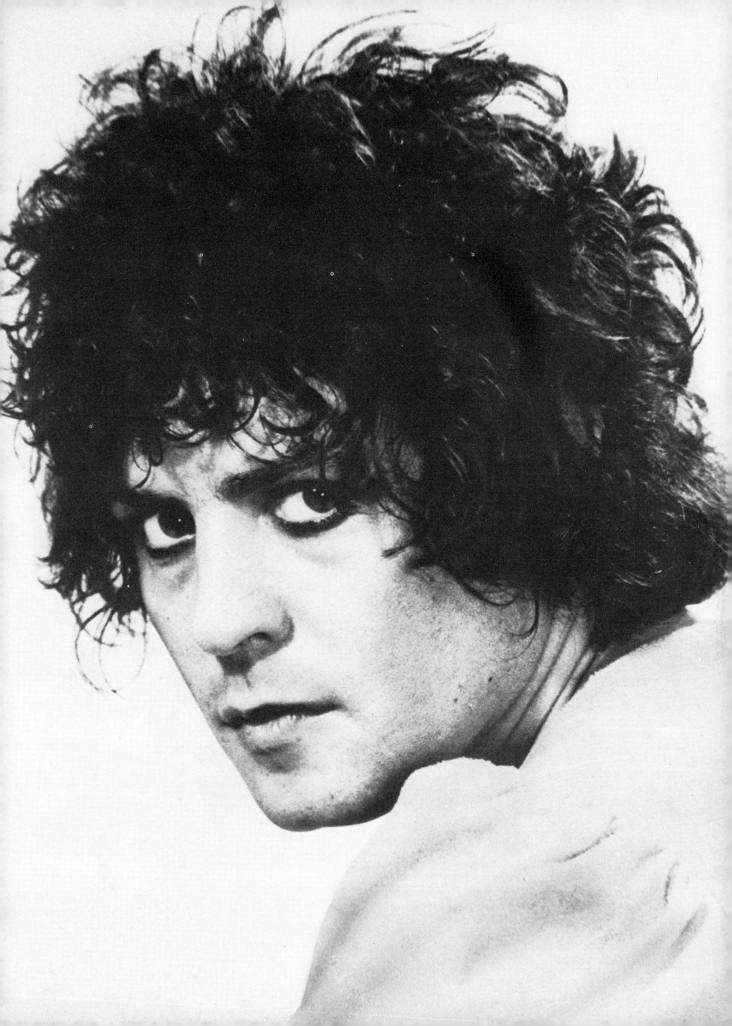

of poetry in his lilting couplets.

Marc would happily talk for hours in this vein, influenced particularly by the writings of Tolkein, creator of 'The Lord Of The Rings', and others who dabbled in myths and magic — popular palliatives during those high-speed, grossly commercial boom-years.

But Bolan watchers noticed a subtle change during 1968 as the imagery grew harsher and less elfin-like in character. Dark forces stirred in his imagination, and the elves became more macho. The woodlands were riven by lightning bolts, and witches in black hats rode broomsticks across his lyrics. There was no doubt Bolan the Bopping Imp was becoming a somewhat peeved pixie.

He released a series of good singles, including 'Debora', 'One Inch Rock', 'Pewter Suitor', 'King Of The Rumbling Spires' and 'By The Light of the Magical Moon' during 1968-69, but while they were well-received by Tyrannosaurus Rex fans, they failed to set the charts alight. Bolan became dispirited, resentful and angry.

When huge success came with 'Ride A White Swan' in 1970, almost overnight the charming pixie seemed in danger of being overwhelmed. The new Bolan was loud, bombastic, and a kaleidoscope of personalities began glistening and breaking out, like a succession of soap bubbles.

He was speeding, tripping on fame, as he was carried away on a tidal wave of all the appreciation he had yearned for. And everything was heightened by intense adulation and hero worship.

He drank and he swore and he boasted. When he talked now of his old poetical imagery, it sounded phoney, cynical and forced. He knew it, he regretted it, but he couldn't stop it. The carefully-wrought flower-power image belonged to the past. The elfin child had grown up. The Bolan of T. Rex was a rock'n'roll punk, out to defend his hard-won territorial gains.

His old boyish charm was distorted into an outrageous effeminacy, calculated to shock, and marred by a double chin that threatened to wreck once-perfect features.

In his third phase, after the 1970-72 era, Marc took stock of himself. Hurt and upset by public and private criticism, he began to cool down and began to restore his prestige. He cut down on drink and cocaine, and rebuilt a shattered private life. The ultimate Bolan contained elements of all his past incarnations. He remained cocksure, and could still anticipate the end of conversation before it had begun. But gone were the grandiose claims for his genius. He was kindly disposed toward the world and he hoped the world forgave him his trespasses.

He accepted with good grace that the hits were fewer and farther between, and even adopted a 'grand old man of rock' stance as he encouraged new bands on his own TV show. The critics took him even less seriously, but he bit his lip and carried on making optimistic albums with the Bolan boogie beat. When they said he was finished, he formed a new band and went out on the road, to wild acclaim.

Towards the end he seemed somehow more vulnerable than he had been before stardom caught him in its grip. The future had arrived before he was ready.

In 1968 Marc Bolan, attempting to look into his destiny, said: "I can't really get turned on to a pop ego thing. God is a good thing, and if I started to believe I was a splinter of God's head I'd be zapped and mown down by lightning. And what good would that be? I'd never get into the charts then!"

It was Bolan's strangest, most accurate prophecy.

A child's imagination, fired by the fear and wonder of everything he sees around him, is a remarkable facility, an inner eye, that is usually stifled or allowed to wither with approaching manhood. Those who retain their imagination and sense of wonder are our poets, lyricists, song-writers, musicians, artists and authors.

Marc Bolan was no angel. He absorbed a modest amount of education at school, but he was worldly wise and picked up most of his information by observation and experience. Restless, impatient, inquisitive, he learnt how to extract information from people and how to motivate them.

"Marc knew how to suck people dry of knowledge," says one of his oldest friends. "He would smile at them and his eyes bored right into them."

When Marc Bolan became a rock superstar in 1971 he seemed to draw a veil of secrecy over his childhood and early career. And the reason was that his confusion of fact and fantasy had become too difficult to unravel.

His imagination, which led to the creation of an array of personalities and images, also led him to grow bored with the past. The present and the future were Marc's constant preoccupations. Suffice to say he had French ancestry, that he studied the Occult and lived in Paris under the

tutelage of a mysterious wizard. It appealed to the press, even if it baffled his friends and parents.

Marc Bolan was born Marc Feld in Hackney Hospital, on 30 September 1947. His parents were Syd and Phyllis Feld. His father was a lorry driver who also took a variety of other jobs, while Phyllis ran a stall in London's Berwick Street market.

Marc also had an older brother called Harry, who processed films for Kodak and later became a long-distance lorry driver. When Marc announced that he didn't want a regular job but wanted to be a pop star, he came under pressure from his dad, who wanted to know why he couldn't be like Harry and get a decent job. But Marc didn't want to work as a film processor, and felt he had more creative things to do in life.

His mother was to support him in his early bid for a career in music. She would slip him the odd five shillings, and even bought him his first guitar for £14. She was to provide a sturdy background of support against much opposition.

From an early age Marc learnt the art of survival and the need to keep his wits about him in a tough environment. He was small and good looking, and swiftly learnt that a speedy riposte and fast escape were the best measures to adopt if he came under attack. In later years he looked back on the days when he helped out on his mother's stall. "It was half a crown for the barrow and half a crown for Marc," he told friends.

He grew up in the Fifties, a decade dominated more by the cinema than television. He'd go regularly to the movies, and found an escape route from suburbia into a world of cowboys, Indians and science fiction. His earliest heroes were film creations like *Mighty Joe Young* and the *Phantom of the Opera*. The time would come when he was able to create his own fantasy images, like the Metal Guru.

He spent his early school days in Stoke Newington, an area of North London where it was still possible to play a whole variety of street games, before the encroaching tide of traffic blocked such activity. There were games like Tin Can Tommy and Knock Down Ginger, but the ones eight-year-old Marc enjoyed most were the mock street battles, with the participants wearing their dads' old army helmets.

Marc was exceptionally bright, but could never concentrate sufficiently on studies and failed his 11-plus, the school examination which was supposed to set the pattern of one's future.

Marc was setting his own patterns however, and had already displayed a keen interest in pop music, to the extent that his father bought him a drum kit when he was only eight. A year later, he was given his first guitar. Whatever Marc wanted to do as a child, he received every encouragement from his parents, and he was to look back on his childhood with great affection. He was to fight a long rearguard-action against encroaching adulthood.

His musical activities were gradually replacing his involvement in gang-warfare, and one of his first groups was a school trio called Susie and the Hoola Hoops. Marc played tea-chest bass, and the singer was a girl called Helen Shapiro. This was in 1959. Two years later Helen Shapiro achieved fame as one of Britain's first child rock-stars, with a string of hits including 'Don't Treat Me Like A Child', 'You Don't Know' and the classic 'Walkin' Back To Happiness'. Her success made a profound impression on him, and he could see a future for himself as an entertainer.

By now he was at William Wordsworth secondary school in North London. Although he noted that the building was named after a poet, there was nothing fanciful about the

occupants, mostly teenage thugs, and as he couldn't beat 'em, he joined them. He wasted his years there, although he was interested in subjects like art and history. It was difficult to concentrate even if he wanted to learn, and what Marc most wanted to know about wasn't on the curriculum.

He loved pop music and fashion, and clothes became as important to him as plunking on his sixteen quid guitar. Marc was a teenager during the Mods and Rockers era, when teenagers were divided into those who dressed sharply in the latest shirts, suits, ties and shoes, on the one hand, and those who wore leather jackets and jeans. Crash helmets and grease weren't Marc's style.

It would be intriguing to know what the other cockney kids made of Bolan, a bright young kid, full of ideas and so swift to respond to circumstances. They may have been dimly aware that he joined in their games to humour them. He may have been an 11-plus drop-out like them, but his sights were always raised a little higher. Marc once said of his pals: "They were sweet kids really. But they were always on their guard. That type's insecure really. They take some time to accept you as one of them."

Marc worked on his mother's stall in the street market, and did all kinds of odd jobs to raise money to spend on clothes. He was impressed by Teddy Boys and the teenage fashions of the late Fifties, mostly American-influenced. But English boys were developing their own, often bizarre ideas of dress, and Marc was swift to emulate the older youths and their experiments with green shoes and baggy trousers.

He developed the art of hanging-out, meeting interesting people in showbusiness and the fashion world. With no practical skills or experience, there didn't seem a lot he could do, apart from go backstage at concerts and into TV studios. But he caught a glimpse of his future.

However, there was one undeniable asset he could utilize — his good looks. Marc was expelled from school when he was 14, as he had stopped attending lessons. "I didn't think they were teaching me the things I wanted to know," he said later. At least he was free to read poetry, practise guitar — and hustle. He used to hang out at an amusement arcade in Stamford Hill, where he made a lot of friends. But many of them turned against him when Marc first tasted a sort of fame.

Town magazine was looking for a model to put on their cover to illustrate an article on the burgeoning Mod movement. Marc was recommended and photographed as representative of his generation. A caption under the article read:

'Where is the goal towards which he is running as fast as his impeccably shod feet can carry him? It is nowhere. He is running to stay in the same place, and he knows by the time he has reached his mid-twenties the exhausting race will be over and he will have lost.'

Not a terribly good prediction, but then even Marc didn't really know what he wanted, and he was certainly not all that keen on being pushed into a career as a model. He was regarded as the smart, handsome local boy who had made good. He modelled suits for the John Temple tailoring chain and also appeared in mail-order catalogues. He found it an eerie experience to see himself as a cut-out dummy in shop windows.

When his parents moved to Wimbledon in South London and Marc was sent to another school, he found it difficult to adjust to the change, and his expulsion followed shortly afterwards. When he wasn't helping his mother in the market or serving coffee at the *2I's*, Soho's home of

HE MARQUISE DE POMPADOUR

rock'n'roll, he was sitting around with friends playing records, or exploring the record shops of Tooting. He built up a working knowledge of jazz and blues as well as pop and rock, and liked to be able to pontificate about the various musicians and their styles.

He found that his brief fame as a Mod on the cover of *Town* had its drawbacks. Kids called him a cissy and their persecution was partly responsible for driving him away from Hill Croft School.

Marc toyed with the idea of becoming an actor and obtained a small part, playing a suitable role as a young delinquent, opposite Sam Kydd in his TV series *Orlando.* "I never took acting seriously" said Marc. "I knew I wanted to do *something*, but that wasn't it."

He filled in time with mundane odd jobs, working in a clothes store in Tooting, washing dishes in a Wimpy Bar — anything to hustle bread. He could work hard, but it wasn't his style. From the age of 14 he believed that his destiny was to be a singing star. It was unlikely that he'd get much encouragement in a Wimpy bar, and he naturally gravitated towards showbusiness and the glamorous people on its periphery, whether they were actors, celebrities, artists, photographers or producers. He knew that his boyish good looks appealed as much to men as to women, and he was never afraid to utilize his attractive qualities, whether it meant going to bed or simply acting as decoration.

If he seemed silent and shy, his mind was working overtime as he looked into his future. He displayed remarkable intuition about people, sharpened by his wide-ranging contacts, and could even project the effects of fame, and how he would change his personality, then settle down and become a mature adult. It wasn't so much a fantasy as a plan for life, and such determination amused those who saw him as just another kid.

But he made friends with another teenager who had faith in him. Allen Warren was the same age as Marc, although he was already forging ahead with his career. Says Allen: "I was the kid presenter on a show produced by Muriel Young called *Five O'Clock Club*. We had all the big stars on the show, like the Rolling Stones and the Beatles. Marc and I lived together when we were 14. I had rented a huge apartment in Lexham Gardens for £35 a week, which was a lot of money in those days."

The flat had fitted carpets and central heating, and Allen was regarded as rather sharp for someone so young. "I forget how we met. He just breezed his way in and we lived together for a while."

Marc used to sit cross-legged on their sitting-room floor playing his own songs with an acoustic guitar. Allen thought he looked like a baby-faced Cliff Richard. "But he was quite pudgy in the face. I had a desk and some 'phones on it, and I thought if I added a couple more 'phones I could be a pop manager. Marc and I agreed that I should be his personal manager, so I had an acetate made of him singing."

The song was a Betty Everett number 'You're No Good' and it was decided that Marc Feld should change his name — to Toby Tyler. "He was about 15 years old then, and I went to a photographer called Mike McGrath. We had some dreadful pictures taken of him in a cap, and I was charged £35. I had the acetate made in Regent Sound Studio in Denmark Street. Then I took the record and pictures round to Rediffusion TV — and they didn't want to know at all! So nothing really happened for the next two years. He drifted out of my flat and out of my life."

The attempt at management had proved a disappointment, but not a disaster. Allen sold his contract

with Marc for £200 to property tycoon David Kirsch, who owned the flat he rented.

One day Kirsch was verbally attacked in his office by Marc's mum. Mrs. Feld wanted to know what he'd been doing for her boy. He thought it was all very funny and said he'd done nothing because he'd put the contract into a filing cabinet and forgotten all about it. But he willingly gave it back and she tore it up.

Allen later observed Marc's career with interest, but from afar. He did not see him again until one day at a party at his house in 1977 when there was an incident.

"I was up in my bedroom talking to Rod Stewart, who had his arms around me, when somebody said : 'I've got a good mind to punch you right in the mouth.' I was shocked but I thought, well I'd be all right because I had Rod with me. So I said 'But why should you want to do that?' And he said 'Because you are Allen Warren and I'm Marc Bolan and you didn't recognize me.' We cuddled and embraced and he said 'I want you to have this'."

Marc gave Allen a James Dean badge he was wearing. "James Dean was his big hero. But I wasn't into wearing badges so I gave it away. Marc once rang me from his house in Barnes and said 'I'm sitting on the loo and reading your autobiography. It's very funny'." They kept in touch as friends.

"He was very reclusive in the early days when he spent six months sitting on my living-room floor. A lot of people thought he was gay, but he wasn't. He was bisexual, but people thought he was only gay.

"He said to me 'I'm gonna be a star.' His arrogance was incredible. He flirted with the gay scene but he was more there for decoration, rather than people taking him home. Gays took an interest in him, and if they could help him get on then he had no qualms about it. When he was 14 he didn't really have an image. His clothes were very traditional sixties, with mohair slacks, and his hair was straight, it wasn't curly at all."

Today Allen Warren is a top society photographer and author of *Nobs & Nosh: Eating with the Beautiful People*. He says that Marc was very much a socialite: "He knew loads of people. The gay world is like the theatre world, with no class distinctions or barriers, as long as you don't tread on anyone's toes."

Life in a prefab in Wimbledon with his parents must have been claustrophobic, even for the diminutive Bolan, and he had to get away, go abroad, explore further than the boundaries of Tooting Broadway. The nearest exciting place was Paris, and he went there with Riggs O'Hara, an actor he had met at the National Theatre.

Marc later wove an elaborate tale about this episode, claiming that he had lived in France for five months and had met a man he described as a wizard. Indeed, he dedicated his first single release to this mysterious and romantic figure, who had demonstrated to Marc the arts of levitation and magic.

While his story was accepted by some of the publicity agents who later flitted in and out of the Bolan story, one of Marc's managers pooh-poohed the very existence of the man, or at least belittled his alleged powers. "Magician? He was just a gay conjuror who could toss a few balls in the air, and fell in love with Marc for the weekend."

Marc decided that fantasy was fun, but that he must first learn how to compose and improve his guitar playing. It was to be his weaponry in the battle for acceptance. He knew he could win most people round with his charm, but he also knew he needed basic skills and plenty of material. He was most impressed by the success of Bob Dylan. If

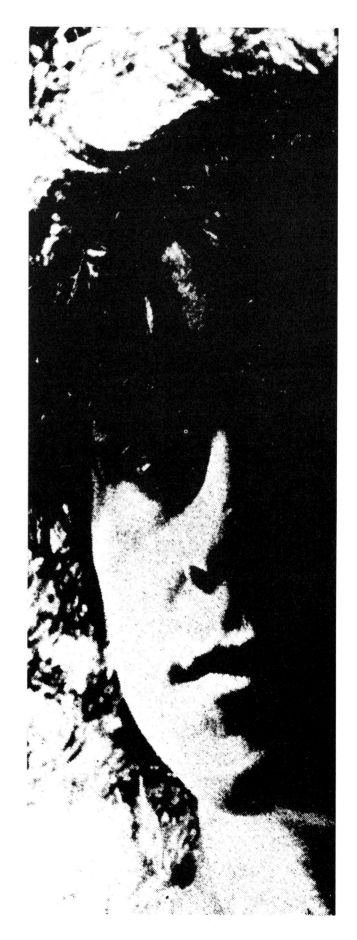

Dylan could sing surrealistic lyrics and convince the world of their significance, then so could poetry-loving Marc Feld from Wimbledon.

Despite the disappointment suffered during his period with Allen Warren, he tried once more to crack the recording world. He failed an EMI recording test, but was taken up by Decca, the British company that seemed to delight in gambling on unknown talent and dropping it just as it was about to blossom.

His first record was 'The Wizard', made with full orchestral backing and produced by Jim Economides and released in 1965. It was a good, unusual performance amidst the dross constantly released by record companies week after week; and it caught the ear of many pop music critics even though it wasn't a hit. Decca had called him Marc Bowland in preference to Marc Feld, and this ultimately turned into Marc Bolan on his subsequent release for Decca, 'The Third Degree', which was coupled with 'San Francisco Poet'.

Marc made his first TV appearance on the cult rock show of the Sixties, *'Ready, Steady Go!'* He performed 'The Wizard', and although Marc sang well, the backing was out of time and did not help create a favourable impression. But in the studio he bumped into a young disc jockey and music-biz face from Dublin, B.P. Fallon, who was to become a life-long friend and publicist-cum-spiritual-advisor.

B.P., or 'Beep' as Marc called him, became an essential part of the fabric of rock society. He spun a web of romantic blarney between the artists, their record companies and journalists. People just liked to have him around as a groover, and his quiet sincerity endeared him to both Marc and his girl friend and wife-to-be, June Child.

"I first met Marc in 1966", says B.P. who has now returned to Dublin after many exhausting years in London. "It was at *Ready, Steady Go,* when Jimi Hendrix was on and played 'Hey Joe'. Marc was there doing 'The Wizard' and Hendrix and Bolan were sizing each other up. Then they started chatting and became pals. With me it was just a grinning and laughing job. We're both little people and we got on well, I suppose. I worked on his promotion, but that was only the visible tip of the iceberg. A lot of the time it was a guru situation. That sounds pompous, but it was down to playing records together and exchanging opinions. The Occult is the wrong word to describe it. He was interested in *normality.* He used to explain that 100 years before the arrival of jet planes, telephones and television, people could communicate with each other over long distances. They could sense if somebody was at home over the other side of a hill before they set off on their journey. Today, people have lost that edge of consciouness, but Marc retained it. He was completely nontechnical. He couldn't figure out tape recorders and couldn't fix a plug. Even changing a light bulb was a big deal, and he couldn't drive a car."

If Marc's appearance on *Ready, Steady Go!* had been a flop, at least it gave him the opportunity of meeting Hendrix, who made a tremendous impression on Marc. He was thrilled by the impact the electric guitar had in such gifted hands, and from then on, even during the acoustic days of Tyrannosauraus Rex, Marc yearned to conquer the power of electricity and strut like a guitar hero.

The following year Marc made a single called 'Hippy Gumbo', which was released on Columbia. It was another flop but got more good reviews. The music business was beginning to learn more about the strange little character who seemed to float in and out of offices and TV studios leaving behind the invariable cry of "Who was *that?*"

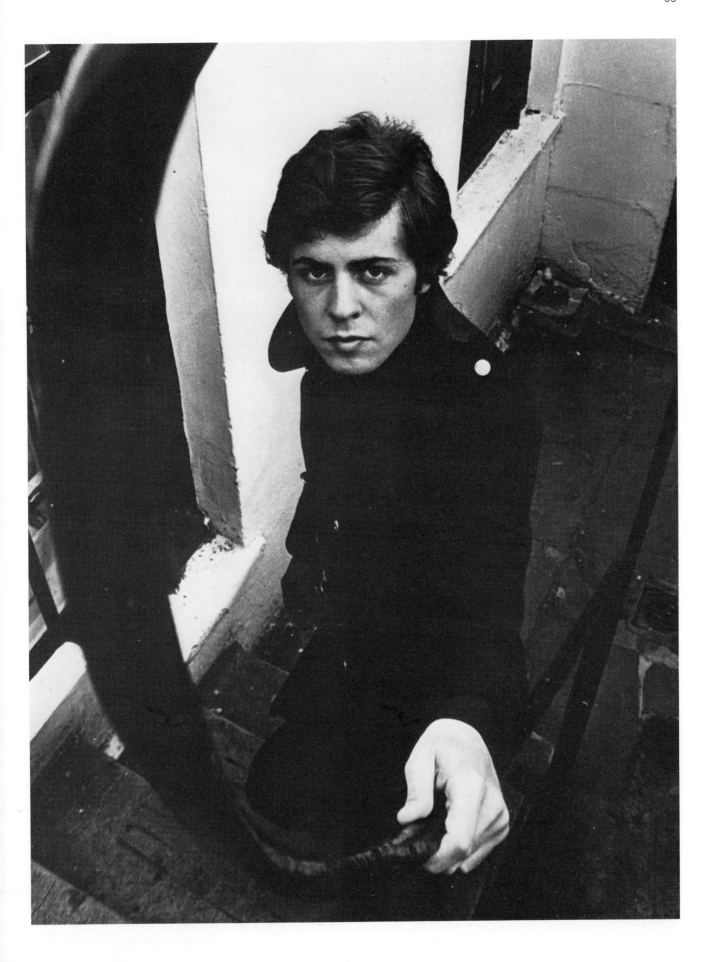

john'

Marc Bolan was to have his first taste of debauched rock'n'roll life in what has been described by its ex-members as the worst band in the world. But John's Children offered Marc valuable experience and a tantalizing glimpse of how an audience could be made to react. It was also an eye-opener to the harsh disappointments and frustrations inherent in a business to which Marc had now become committed. His days as a model and bit-part actor were set aside and buried in the past. His attempts at a solo career had met with failure. He would now plunge himself into a band and absorb everything it had to offer.

John's Children was a somewhat camp, mock violent, mock flower-power and throughly bizarre set-up which presaged Punk Rock's desperate measures by a good ten years. In England they had one minor hit 'Desdemona' (Track), which Marc wrote, which was banned by the BBC because of one offending line: 'Lift up your skirt and fly.'

But in Germany they caused a sensation. Their antics on a tour with the Who caused them to be sacked from the show by the Who's manager, Kit Lambert, and also induced the German police to turn fire hoses on them. The band were drunk, rude and arrogant, and even gentle Marc Bolan became seduced by the air of dangerous mayhem.

The total contrast in music and lifestyle that was adopted by Marc in Tyrannosaurus Rex becomes all the more understandable on delving into the activities of John's Children.

The group evolved out of a series of chance meetings that became a projection of showbusiness fantasies. Two of the members, singer Andy Ellison and drummer Chris Townson, had been at boarding school together and they met up with bass player John Hewlett.

Chris was then a drop-out and wanderer. He once hitch-hiked to France, was jailed for vagrancy, and came back to England with just a threepenny bit in his pocket. He used the coin to make a 'phone call to John Hewlett who said: "I'm glad you are back, there's a gig for the band tonight." It was on this casual and haphazard basis that the band developed.

Despite their laissez-faire attitude they knew they wanted to present an attractive image to the world, and their lead guitarist was unceremoniously booted out, to be replaced by Marc Bolan.

Andy Ellison, who later worked with a group called Radio Stars, remembered Marc when he joined John's Children. "He was always very quiet in those days. He totally changed when he became a star. I remember going over to see him at his parents' house in Wimbledon, near the stadium, which was just like a box. It was a prefab I think. He used to cook us mushrooms and we'd rehearse and write songs."

On the road with the band Marc quietly got on with writing songs. "While everybody else was shooting their mouths off and shouting, he would sit and write strings of words on bits of paper. All the songs on his first solo album 'My People Were Fair' were originally written for John's Children. He was also our lead guitarist, and he played a very simple but powerful style which suited the group.

children

"He once made a big silver screen out of tinfoil to put around the amplifiers so it would reflect his feedback on gigs. He was totally into Jimi Hendrix at that time, and he loved the electric guitar, so I don't know why he went back to acoustic guitar when he formed Tyrannosaurus Rex. I think the reason was basically because he lost all his equipment when he left the group. It all went back to Track Records, and all he had left was an acoustic guitar with a broken neck which he used for two years. He was stuck with acoustic when people began to like it, and he couldn't change for a long time."

Andy and Chris both remember the night when the band played at the *Technicolour Dream*, a huge psychedelic festival at Alexandra Palace in North London, (now burnt down).

Says Andy: "Marc put his guitar on his head and left it feeding back for the whole of our twenty minute set. I don't know how he kept a straight face! I was running around shouting and throwing feathers in the air, and Chris, our drummer, was smashing up his kit. We went down great. The audience was totally bewildered and there was another group playing at the same time at the far end. Marc started whipping his guitar and amplifier with chains. He was into heavy metal before anybody else. After a gig like that Marc would be very bouncy for half an-hour afterwards and then gradually he would go back into a quiet mood."

Chris Townson, who along with Keith Moon and Kenny Jones, has the rare distinction of being one of the Who's drummers (albeit while Keith was incapacitated by rupture), always wanted to play drums to the best of his ability, but found John's Children was not exactly the most musical of bands.

The first time Chris met Marc Bolan was at the John's Children Club, in Leatherhead. It was after they had disposed of their lead guitarist, Geoff McLelland. Chris:

"In our estimation Geoff was a bit limp. We didn't consider he had any power. But he had lots of personality and he was a bit of a clown. On stage though, he looked like a chicken. His best trick was being able to fake a faint. He'd turn white and just fall off the stage. He did that one night so we could finish the gig early and go off to do another one and earn some more money. It was at the Ricky Tick Club in Windsor. We apologised to the promoters and said we were sorry but our guitarist was ill and we'd have to go. It was an old trick and it worked!"

Marc may not have been any good at faking fits, but he was certainly better looking, and an obviously gifted songwriter. "I liked his songs right away, and they seemed very structured. Marc was very quiet and not at all flamboyant as he later became. I got the feeling he wasn't at ease with us. Andy, me and John were different. Andy and I had been to boarding school together from the age of 13. John was the leader and supposed to be the bass player. But musically the band was atrocious. It was the worst band in the world - the worst I've ever seen in my life. John couldn't play bass to save his life, and my drumming was not much better - it consisted mainly of smashing up the kit. I couldn't even keep time. But I used to tune Marc's guitar for him before we went on stage, which irritated and offended him. He never bothered to tune it himself. His guitar produced a horrible muddy blurge of sound, and I wanted him to play like Pete Townshend. It was all slightly ludicrous. But we had a lot of fun. As long as we could pose, look flash and jump about, we were happy. Marc's attitude was 'If you can't beat 'em, join 'em.' He was quite happy with us, but he didn't hang around after gigs. We thought

TRACK RECORD

john's children DESDEMONA

that was the most important part. Get the gig out of the way and start looning about. We had outrageous parties and were totally obnoxious to people."

John's Children has the most astonishing underground reputation in Europe and America, and yet Chris felt the band was virtually non-functional. "Now, my hair would stand on end at the thought of such a band flying off to Germany and actually doing gigs and appearing on TV. After Marc left I took over on lead guitar and we got the roadie, who'd never played an instrument before, to play drums. That epitomized John's Children as a band. And the roadie insisted on having a double drum kit which he thrashed around and knocked over.

"We did three numbers, which was all we knew, and then just smashed everything up for half an hour with John and Andy having a fight. I learned the three numbers pretty well, and when we got to 'Day Tripper' that was the signal to jump into the audience. When he was with us Marc enjoyed himself doing that sort of thing, but it was not part of his overall strategy for a musical career."

It's not surprising perhaps that Marc tended to draw a veil over his period with the band, and was particularly tight-lipped about their treatment of his material. Years later Chris Townson was honest and contrite about the affair.

"We butchered his numbers."

The band were delighted when they appeared to blow the Who off stage during their tour of Germany in 1967 — the year of Flower Power and psychedelia. But it was not exactly a musical battle, more a case of up-staging. And it led to the most horrific scenes, with Bolan and friends virtually re-enacting Dunkirk in their escape from Europe.

"I don't know who ever thought of putting a band like us on with the Who," says Chris. "We actually stopped the Who from playing one night. The police would not allow them on after we had finished."

This incident took place in Nuremburg, inside a huge theatre. "We were playing away when Andy started smashing chairs and giving the Nazi salute. And he shouted 'Come on everybody, start smashing up chairs.' Bolan had a huge length of chain he'd got from somewhere and was beating the floor. The next thing I remember there were hordes of people coming on stage, and this huge German in a tee shirt started kissing me."

Chris and Marc ran back to their dressing rooms and began packing bags, John burst in, grabbed the bags and threw them aside shouting "Get out!" It was almost too late. The police came chasing after the band down the corridor. they managed to grab Andy Ellison who they recognised as the chief chair-smasher. He was booted in the crutch by the police as the group desperately fought their way to a waiting Bentley.

"People began banging on the car roof and the police brought out the water cannons. We went flat out for the border, and we never say any of our clothes or gear again."

The band were breathless with excitement and hysterical laughter broke out in the car as they roared through the night. But behind them they had left chaos and a very angry Who management. "We had stolen the show, but it was nothing to do with music," said Chris. "We never went back to Germany after that."

The police had laid into Andy with such vigour that he had to go to a doctor the following day to have his neck straightened. The whole episode had the effect of bringing the band closer together and Marc felt he was much more involved. As the car took them homeward, Marc began to invent a play for the amusement of his fellow passengers,

THE CHILDREN GET WHAT THEY'RE WANTING

MEET John's Children, the group whose latest disc is entitled "Just What You Want, Just What You'll Get." And the Children are getting what they want—success in the charts. John himself (second left on picture) explains: "Provocative people who get on in life are just like babies. If you cry, you get picked up. We're a bit like that."

JOHN'S CHILDREN — FIRST OF THE ANTI-LUST GROUPS

JOHN'S Children, who make their chart debut this week with their own composition " Just What You Want " (Columbia) are described by their manager Simon Napier Bell (also the Yardbirds' manager) as the first of the " anti-lust " groups.

With the exception of lead guitarist Marc Bolan from Wimbledon the group all come from Leatherhead in Surrey where they manage their own club, the Bluesette.

Simon Napier, who enjoys sticking pins in the more self-righteous and exaggerated concept that the pop scene is now a hot-bed of drugs, immorality and degradation, declares the group a permanent thorn in pop-pomposity!

" They have already had a hit in the U.S. charts with 'Smash Blocked,' " Simon told me. " I wrote it and it was nothing to do with drugs or drink," he added indignantly, "it was about

By KEITH ALTHAM

illicit sex! " We came down against it.

The second of the group's "anti-lust" songs was " Not The Kind Of Girl You'd Take To Bed " which was an " anti-drug " song that Simon had turned down by the recording company who were apparently shocked any group should be so moral!

" Their next single is ' Thomas Abeckett,' " said Simon. " We decided to play safe with this and get right away from drugs and sex and into a good healthy murder. They wrote it themselves and it's all about a fella who goes mad and begins playing funerals in his back garden! "

On stage the group all use " Jordan "

Newcomers to the Charts

equipment especially made for them in the U.S. and only used by top American groups like the Mama's and Papa's and the Turtles. They wear white stage suits and gold medallions although Simon is not sure why.

" I discovered John Hewlett, Chris Townson and Andy Ellison in prison on a vagrancy charge while I was on holiday in St. Tropez," says Simon. " You might say they were professional vagrants. I bailed them out and discovered they were a group, and one of the conditions of my bailing anyone out is that they work for me for three years."

Replaced lead

I spoke to folk-singer Marc Bolan who lately replaced the lead guitarist, as they were rehearsing in London on Friday.

" We are writing and arranging all our own material on stage," said Marc, " and although I still hope to record independently as a solo artist, as far as this group is concerned Andy is lead and sings on the disc.

" Our club, The Bluesette, is a knock-out—we choose all our artists. Last night we had Graham Bond and next week Simon Dupree.

" Apart from Andy, who is 21, we are all 19." Simon describes his group as " completely arrogant, cripplingly honest, totally naive and four good clean healthy lads who sound like the Who plus blues! "

A powerful sort of combination!

'STRAWBERRY' is too far out, says John

THE STRANGEST thing about John's Children is that their line-up today—only five weeks after the release of their hit record "Just What You Want"—is different from what it was when they recorded it.

Their guitarist Jeff McClelland — after eight months with the group — left just after they made this, their second record. They now have singer Marc Bolan with them.

Marc feels slightly uncom-

fortable that he didn't contribute to the record, but apart from that is very happy because the responsibility of being a solo singer was b e g i n - ning to get a bit much. J o h n ' s Children are not just a new name to the chart but to the scene as a whole, having been formed not quite a year.

● JOHN

"We can't stand the musical scene at the moment," says John whom the group are named after. "All these dreadful records like that Harry Secombe thing, and Vince Hill. What a drag it is.

"But honestly British record buyers are very wary. They didn't buy our first record 'Smashed, blocked,' because it was too · way out—but in America it was a hit.

"And 'Strawberry Fields'— there's another example of something too far ahead for the public to accept. You've only got to look at the chart to see the way things are going."

On stage, John's Children do mostly their own material. They play pianos backwards, use odd lighting, scream and have six foot silver metal screens. These screens are very useful to create certain visual effects and fold up after use. They just take a bit of effort to carry around but that, say John's Children, is just one of those things.

acting out the role of a young pop-star being propositioned by a manager complete with cries of "My boy."

The group could not afford to fly back to England so they arrived in Ostende to catch the night ferry. They had plenty of money and a lot of time to spare. The party split up and scattered round town in search of booze and women.

"I saw Marc wobbling down the street, while I was busy talking to a girl selling sweets. I ended up buying this huge pile of sweets," remembers Chris. "We all got drunk and the inevitable happened. A big German pushed past and I said something about 'Wot, no manners?' and he started a fight. I was so drunk that every time I took a swing at him I missed. The next thing that happened was me waking up on the ferry. I was told that both Marc and I had been thrown onto the boat."

They had been rescued by Andy. John Hewlett, who led this disreputable bunch of Children had been legless throughout and had been powerless to help.

"It really was awful," thinks Chris. "We were abusive and obnoxious on the ferry boat. I saw Marc sitting cross legged in the lounge reciting pornographic poetry while all the passengers with their children were trying to eat dinner. We arrived back in England with torn clothes, hangovers and black eyes. I dropped Marc off at his prefab in Wimbledon." His parents must have hoped that Marc would return to a quiet life on the barrows as they surveyed the state of the wanderer.

Although Marc had seen how an audience could be goaded and manipulated into a reaction, he had also seen how the public could be coldly indifferent and audiences could stay away.

One of the band's earliest performances was at a hall in Watford. Marc prepared for the excitement ahead by drinking two bottles of wine to ensure he had plenty of reserves of courage and energy. "We were all very drunk before the curtain went up," said Chris. Slowly the curtains rose, to reveal a depressing sight. "There was nobody there. We were all shattered. We played two numbers, and then a guy said: 'That's enough. Get off.' It was Marc's first gig with us. There was literally not a soul there, except for a girl in a leather jacket chewing gum, who took one look at us and walked away. It was a disaster from beginning to end."

"John's Children was great fun, but it was the loudest and worst band in the world and we often sat around in a little circle and cried, we felt so sorry for ourselves."

It was remarkable that Bolan put up with so much hysteria and violence and showed his patience and adaptability. Says Townson: "I can't believe Marc thought it was what he really wanted. But he was never really in our confidence. He wore white clothes like the rest of us, but he always made sure he had a black motif somewhere on his tee shirt. We would do anything we were told. But he wouldn't."

There was friction within the band one day when Marc eventually let slip his true feelings. He told the band: 'I'll make it one day — but not with this lot.' There was not much they could say, as they were playing all Marc's compositions, like 'Sara Crazy Child', 'Desdemona', and 'Horrible Breath'.

The band produced one album, called 'Orgasm', which purported to be a 'live' performance with the sound of ecstatic audiences cheering on the boys and shrieking 'John!' There were rumours that the concert was a fake.

"Are you kidding?" says Townson. "They were cheering for the Beatles. It was the soundtrack of one of their films. They were yelling for John Lennon."

You could always tell when Marc Bolan was angry. He seethed in silence. The smile vanished, to be replaced by tight, pursed lips, and his eyes grew darker. Thunder clouds hovered over his brow. Marc was undoubtedly angry with John's Children. And it wasn't because they had lured him into drunken brawls in the Fatherland. He was most peeved at their treatment of one of his songs, one of his proudest writing achievements. The years of sitting cross legged on the floors of various crash pads, strumming his guitar and scribbling lyrics, were beginning to get results. He was gaining respect as a song writer during an era when the phenomenon of the pop musician as composer was rapidly gaining credence. There was Bob Dylan, Ray Davies and Pete Townshend, and now Marc Bolan.

"Well why not?" thought Marc. The problem was how to get his songs treated with respect and performed in the best possible way. The answer, of course, was to form his own group. The time was rapidly approaching when he had to strike a blow for independence and become his own boss.

To outside observers at the time, why Marc grew so disillusioned with John's Children was a mystery. After all, they had provided him with a ready-made group and a considerable amount of publicity. The band had welcomed him, and yet Bolan remained cool.

He wanted to form a group that would be better than John's Children. He was still officially a member of the Children when he placed an advertisement in *Melody Maker* seeking musicians for an audition. To emphasise

his ambition he named his new group after the largest living creature to stalk the earth — Tyrannosaurus Rex!

It was a time of tremendous excitement. It was the year when the culture and lifestyle of San Francisco spread out and reached the whole Western World. It was a drug-based culture of freedom and experiment, a heady mixture of art, mysticism and music. The young hippies were a natural progression from the beatniks of previous generations, brought to fruition in the sunshine of California. The artists and musicians of London were swept away by the whole concept and responded with their own interpretation of events. The jingle of bells worn around the neck, and the fragrance of burning joss sticks, brought a pleasant madness to the old city.

The crude exploitation and public mockery of Flower Power was swift. Never was a movement more quickly tarnished and crushed. Significantly 1967 was also the year when 'skinheads' were first seen on the London streets, a working class rebellion against the inexplicable aberrations of the essentially middle-class 'long-'aired 'ippies'. This was taking airs and graces too far. Even at the *Technicolour Dream*, where John's Children had played, local youths had attacked the so-called hippies - kids who had put on paisley shirts and the like for the occasion — queuing outside the hall.

Whatever the turmoil and confusion caused by the Hippie Revolution and its impact on society at large, (and it affected everything from the *Carry On* Films of the period to the designs in the local highstreet stores), its most important contribution was to create a climate where British rock music could progress:

It was the age of experimentation, and the results were a fantastic plethora of different styles, as the old blues and R & B bands changed into gaudy new butterflies like Dantalian's Chariot, Pink Floyd, Soft Machine, Cream and the Jimi Hendrix Experience.

Tyrannosaurus Rex fitted perfectly into this new world of high hopes and aspirations. But there was a false start before Marc found his feet. His first inclination was to form a powerful electric band. He had been inspired by the success of Tomorrow, an excellent band with Steve Howe on guitar, which had provided the scene with one of its first anthems - the classic single 'My White Bicycle', which heavily featured the use of Wah-Wah Pedal. Marc fancied himself in the same sort of role, and figured it only needed a bit of human chemistry — or magic — to get such a band off the ground.

It was typical of the age that the first contender for his new venture should be called Steve Peregrine Took. He had 'took' his name from Tolkien's epic cycle of stories which everybody dipped into but claimed to have read - *The Lord of the Rings*. It perfectly suited Marc's interest in poetry and magical being to have a Peregrine Took in the band, on drums. Two other musicians were procured through the ad Marc put in the *Melody Maker* but they were an odd couple who proved entirely incompatible with the Bolan-Took axis. Without a proper rehearsal they played their first gig at the *Electric Garden* in Covent Garden. This was a dark cavernous place which later became Middle *Earth*. Baffled Covent Garden porters who then operated the old fruit and vegetable market were convinced that human sacrifice took place inside and once stormed its portals.

They were right in a way. A sacrifice was offered up to the gods of rhythm the night that Marc Bolan unveiled his new band.

"It was the worst thing anybody had seen in their lives,"

48

said someone who was there. "You'd never see another gig as bad as that. Marc believed it would all happen by magic. It was all because he'd met that magician in Paris. He thought he could get a few people along who had never met each other before and have a magic gig. They were barracked and thrown off. It completely destroyed Marc's ego. He was totally fucked by it. Later he said he didn't want anything to do with electric musicians. He was going to sit on a rug and play by himself."

Marc had been ten years too soon for punk with his policy of giving audiences a string of titles and fingers-crossed jamming. The final blow came when Track Records asked for the return of Marc's gear, since he had departed from John's Children. Debts were mounting, and sheer economic necessity dictated the birth of the Tyrannosaurus Rex duo, with Marc on a six quid guitar and Steve on a pair of salvaged bongos. The drum kit had gone to pay Steve's rent, and the world's cheapest rock band set off on a magical mystery tour into the future.

In answer to the question: what had happened to the big electric band the would-be fans had been led to expect?, Bolan smiled: "No man, it's just the two of us now."

He explained: "I freaked out of the John's Children thing. I had no bread — nothing. Then I met Steve. He stayed at my flat and there were some bongos lying around. He started playing to the songs I was writing. Then John Peel played a record called 'Hippy Gumbo' I had made two years ago on his Perfumed Garden show. I went to meet John and we started doing things at *Middle Earth* for two pounds ten a gig. I didn't know how big we could get. I just enjoyed playing. It made me feel happy. We're not stars or anything, but it's better than starving on five shillings a week."

John Peel, the legendary poll-winning deejay who has done so much to help the careers of countless rock musicians over the years, was an early supporter of Tyrannosaurus Rex, and their association with him seemed to epitomise the ear of self-help and home-made music. The appeal of the duo was its simplicity. They bought their instruments on the cheap from Woolworths, and like a pair of pixies sitting on the floor strumming and rattling clay pot bongos, they were almost a folk group.

John Peel had lost his position at the old Radio London station and was in need of work, so he and Marc began playing gigs together at *Middle Earth*. John played the latest hip records and Tyrannosaurus Rex played acoustic unamplified music between sets. John was to be a loyal supporter. When he eventually found employment at the BBC, with Radio One replacing the old pirate stations, he helped Marc get several radio sessions.

When Marc died John Peel said: "Marc was unique in that he went from being the idol of the flower children to the idol of the teenyboppers, something nobody else had done. His early music was unique too. You couldn't see where it had come from, nor where it was going.

"He was a very amiable bloke, but I think we were all aware that he had a harder edge to his character which came to the surface later on. It's rather sad that when things started to slip away from him he started to build up myths around himself. I personally mourned the passing of the earliest Marc Bolan."

Somewhere along the line the relationship between Marc and Peel had turned sour. Maybe John felt miffed when his old friend took off into stardom and left him behind. But Marc was to leave a lot of people behind over the years, as he had done right from his earliest days as Toby Tyler.

But in 1967-68 the duo and mentor gave substance and flavour to the hippie dreams of brotherhood. Despite the sneers and cynicism of a later generation of critics, there were moments during that period when it really seemed as if the musical fraternity at least were going to change the world for the better.

For many people one of the most enduring memories of the period was of sitting on the grass in the sunshine, smelling the sweet clouds of cannabis, observing the multi-coloured beads and bells and kaftans drifting by, and listening to Marc Bolan singing 'Debora' with Steve beating a busy accompaniment.

They played everywhere — at all the colleges and open-air rock-festivals, from Woburn to the Isle of Wight. John often provided transport in his 'Peel Mobile', a tiny van loaded with records. It was usually impossible to see Marc over the heads of the crowds or even the edge of the stage. If you were lucky you could see his curly head thrown back, his eyes closed, mouth open, and bare arms strumming furiously.

Fans were thoroughly intrigued in particular by Marc's vocal style, which had developed into a highly original mixture of blues-passion and folk-whimsy. He had a strange neighing vibrato which people delighted in imitating at parties.

'Debora' was released as the group's first single on the Regal Zonophone label and was produced by Tony Visconti, who was also a key man in the recording affairs of David Bowie. Visconti, an American who later married singer Mary Hopkins, discovered Tyrannosaurus Rex at *Middle Earth* in 1968, and fell in love with the unlikely combination.

He recorded their first album, the classic 'My People Were Fair And Had Sky In Their Hair... But Now They're Content To Wear Stars On Their Brows', which was one of the longest LP titles of all time, and was invariably shortened to 'My People Were Fair.'

The same year Marc released a driving single of 'One Inch Rock' which proved that despite all the imagery of elves, satyrs, and pixies, he was still a rock'n'roller at heart. It was well received and was a minor hit. The Bolan Steamroller was beginning to gain momentum, but the hippies weren't really buying enough of his albums to match the loyalty he was beginning to inspire. From ten pounds a gig, the band had gone up to £150 a night and they released their second album in November the same year, 'Prophets, Seers and Sages And the Angels of The Ages'. This included another version of 'Debora' (sometimes spelt with a final 'h' and sometimes without).

The titles on these albums summed up Bolan's delight in word-play and the torrent of ideas that were sparking his imagination. If he didn't know the meaning of words, he'd make them up, alter them to give them a Bolan flavour of what he thought poetry should sound like. He was creating his own language, just as language was fashioned from the Neanderthal grunts of our forefathers. There were tales of 'The Travelling Tragition', and 'Salamanda Palaganda' and wonderful titles like 'Dwarfish Trumpet Blues', 'Frowning Atahuallpa (My Inca Love)' and 'Trelawney Lawn'.

It was all very sweet, touching and convincing, and there was no doubt nobody believed in it more firmly than the author, one M. Bolan.

But behind the 'tragition' lurked Bolan the practical, a cheerful hustler who realised that he couldn't do everything on his own. He knew that somewhere along the line he needed people to fix the promotion, the radio and TV exposure; to unlock the key to bigger record sales. Loyal friends alone were not enough.

CHAPTER FIVE

Marc habitually wore an old black and red striped school blazer and his hair had become a mass of corkscrew curls which framed the famous smile. As he trudged around the offices of agents and managers, people found him amusing and irresistable.

And among those who fell for his charm was the girl who was to share such an important chunk of his life, who helped steer him toward stardom, and who eventually became Mrs. Marc Bolan.

June Child was working in the office of Blackhill Enterprises, the top management company run by Andrew King and Peter Jenner. They looked after the affairs of artists like Pink Floyd and Roy Harper and also put on the famous free festivals in Hyde Park. Marc was a huge fan of Syd Barrett (then the Floyd's composer, singer and guitarist) and approved of their hippie management team.

Marc visited the Blackhill office and invited them to see him play a gig at Ealing College with Steve Took.

Says June: "Andrew and I went to see him, and he had a tiny AC30 amplifier and a bent coat hanger for a mike stand. He was singing away and the audience loved him. He was a scruffy little sod in his striped school blazer and his mum's old boots with zips up the side." Two hours after a business meeting with Marc, he called the office; the Blackhill team thought there must be some problem with the contract they had offered, so June got on a train back to the Wimbledon prefab where they had met earlier in the day. Marc met her on the doorstep and said: "I have to talk to you. I'm in love with you." And he greeted her with a love poem he had already written.

54

Says June: "We sat on his mum's lawn, and had a bowl of muesli in the sun and just talked and talked. It was extraordinary. I was much older than him. He was 20 and I was almost 25. I went back to the office and told them what happened and Peter and Andrew just laughed and said 'Come on, Child!' "

It was the start of a relationship that was to last three years and spanned the most exciting and successful period in Marc's career. June was already living with a boyfriend and she told him she was leaving. The boyfriend was understandably stunned to hear he was being pushed aside for an unknown rival that June had only met the day before. But she grabbed her tooth-brush and overnight bag and set off for Wimbledon.

Marc told his mother he was off to Brighton for a few days, but instead he jumped into June's van and they drove to Wimbledon Common where they set up home, living in the van on the Common for four days.

"We lived, ate and slept in the van where we parked. It was unbelievable." Then she found a cold-water flat at 57 Blenheim Crescent, in Notting Hill, a tiny Dickensian attic, and the couple moved in.

There was no bath and just one gas hob with two burners. All the water for washing had to be boiled in a kettle but the rent was only £3.8s.6d. a week. (£3.45p)

"And some weeks we had difficulty getting that together," says June.

Marc needed somewhere to practise guitar and write songs, so he curtained off a tiny cubby hole and sat there for hours, writing the songs that would eventually get them out of their impoverished circumstances. June made him pots of his favourite Jasmine tea. Eventually, when the first Performing Rights Society royalty cheques started to come in — greeted with loud cheers — they were able to take larger rooms on the floor below, and Marc could expand into a larger cubby hole, grandly called the Music Room. It was labelled 'Toadstool Studio', and was equipped with an ancient tape recorder.

This hideaway was where Marc wrote 'Ride A White Swan' and many of his other hits. June: "It was a very good time. I was incredibly happy. It was the first time Marc had lived away from home, and he loved the freedom."

June carried on working at Blackhill by day and at night came home to brew the tea, and in her spare time made her own lampshades. She inflated a balloon, coated it with light material, then let down the baloon and withdrew it, leaving a perfect globe ready for painting and decoration.

Marc too joined in this cottage industrial enterprise and helped make Christmas and Greeting cards, with messages in his curious spidery handwriting and phonetic spelling.

"He was like George Bernard Shaw — trying to introduce his own phonetic spelling," says June. Many friends who received cards and letters from June and Marc in this period still treasure them, and June has boxes of poems and love letters stored away.

Gradually she found herself working more and more for Marc's musical enterprise, helping to arrange dates and taking care of business. He began to work four nights a week, for £25 a session. "That was good money then, so I decided to leave Blackhill," she said. "They said I took his contract with me, but in fact he never signed with them. Then he recorded 'Debora' and it got to number 28 in the chart. It was wonderful!"

The name of the game was self-sufficiency, which the hippies were practising long before it became a Seventies vogue word. But despite the vegetarianism and non-

smoking, non-drinking stance, Marc never really saw himself as a hippie. He was filled with a driving ambition that made June realise he would make it, with or without her help. It caused some tensions, that would eventually manifest themselves in rows, but at first they enjoyed great happiness, and in between weaving fantasy stories about himself and his life, he would occasionally own up to June about his past deeds.

For example, she read and believed in the story that he had spent five months in France, living with the famous wizard. It had even been chronicled in a girls' comic book story about Marc, with drawings of him sitting at the feet of the wizard.

Eventually he told her that the trip had lasted three days and the wizard was a guy who had fallen in love with him. They were pictured together sitting on a boat on the Seine.

He also told her why he had left John's Children - he was fed up with not being the lead singer. He wanted his songs done properly, but had been cast in the role of guitarist.

"He knew what he wanted. If he hadn't found me he would have found somebody else. It was totally unconscious, but he set up a gravitational field which drew people towards him to help him. He was a Libran, and they are sensitive, creative, self-indulgent and beautiful people."

Life changed for the happy couple, as it was bound to, when Marc began to earn more money and his fame grew. When they earned a few pounds a week, they invited friends round to share a bottle of wine. They'd sit and talk and play records. When the cash began rolling in, Marc, who had never smoked cigarettes, found he could indulge in more fashionable vices, like inhaling cocaine. Mixed with copious amounts of brandy, which the cocaine enabled him to drink without suffering the normal symptoms of drunkenness, it sometimes changed his personality into something altogether less pleasant.

It was a great moment when the first 'real' money arrived in the Bolan household. On Friday they faced the possibility of being thrown out for rent arrears. They owed around £30, so June took Marc's beloved old 17th century French guitar and deposited it at the pawnbroker.

The following Monday a cheque arrived 'out of the blue' from the Performing Rights Society, for the huge sum of £680. It seemed like a fortune to the impoverished lovers and June dashed back to the pawnbroker to get the guitar out of hock; she then paid off the rent.

"But we never felt broke!" says June. "Marc never had a bank account, and there was never an overdraft to worry us. We spent our evenings together, or with friends. We had no TV for God knows how long."

Somehow they managed to get a lot done with the minimum of facilities. "Marc didn't feel he was a hippie. He was a chess player who never actually learned to play chess."

Marc began to develop a reputation for being a sharp businessman quite early on in his career, but a lot of the thrust was engendered by June making the right phone calls to the right people.

"He was intuitive in a business sense, and he needed me as A.N. Other. I have no false illusions about him not being able to do it all without me. He would have done it anyway. It sounds high-falutin', but it was his destiny. He needed someone to deal with the practicalities. It sounds very callous, but that's how it worked out; he was a very happy man in those days, but he wasn't later."

One example of June's practical assistance was when an early hit — June thinks it was 'Hot Love' — got stuck in the

chart. By the sales figures they received from the record company, they knew it should have gone up a few places. But when it stayed still, Marc 'went spare' and became beside himself with rage. He couldn't understand why his record hadn't gone up when it was outselling others that were higher in the hit parade.

June tried to explain that the compilers of the charts had probably made a mistake, but he insisted that she phone one of the music newspapers concerned and register a complaint. It was explained that there had been a miscalculation and the next week the record dutifully went up a few places.

It was not just pride on Marc's part. He knew that without a higher placing he couldn't get an appearance on BBC TV's *Top Of The Pops*. That meant the record would probably drop of its own volition, and media interest would be lessened.

"Until the record jumped into its proper place my life was absolute hell", says June. Marc shouted that he didn't want people to make mistakes, but when he was happy with his placing all became sweetness and light.

Despite his increasing tendency to throw tantrums, June felt protective towards him and could see how vulnerable he was. Sometimes he would come home and cry if someone had upset him or let him down. He cared for a wide cross-section of people, but he gradually became more cynical over the years. June saw it as a slow erosion of his trust and faith in people in the business.

"When you attain his heights it's difficult not to become cynical. But he became suspicious to the point where he questioned everybody's motives and even the air they breathed. It was a process that was hard to define and stop."

Whatever private pressures were building up on Bolan, the public saw a different picture, of a cult figure trembling on the brink of stardom.

There was a whirl of activity as he took a great leap forward into the Seventies, riding on a gusher of hits. While elitists thought he was selling out, pandering to the masses, most record buyers simply welcomed what seemed to be the best new face and the most excitingly different music they'd seen and heard in a long time.

But there were a few dramas and tragedies in store for Marc before he attained his long dreamt of stardom. Friends couldn't always keep up the pace he set, and some fell by the wayside. Worse was in store for one of his closest allies.

Marc remained strong and resolute. His boldest step was to take himself and Steve Took to America and seek instant success and recognition. America had proved the salvation for most of Britain's top rock bands. Once they had played all the venues there were to play at home, and pushed their earnings to the local limits, they could either turn to America or face slow death and extinction. The States offered a vast new audience of super enthusiastic fans, and enormous radio, TV and record outlets. The Americans welcomed the new British invaders and made heroes of many a group from Pink Floyd to the Who.

But they found Marc Bolan too hard to understand or accept. The crazed diminutive character didn't seem to fit into any category, and was trying too hard to cross over into too many areas. Was he a poet, a hippie, a rock'n'roller or a pop star? Was he serious? The humour and make-believe inherent in Tyrannosaurus Rex had little appeal for Americans en masse, and it was to be a source of great permanent disappointment, though he always pretended it wasn't.

In 1969 Bolan released another single, 'Pewter Suitor' for Regal Zonophone, and a beautiful album 'Unicorn', still regarded by many fans as Bolan's best work. The royalties coming in from the previous 'Prophets, Seers And Sages' album enabled the duo to expand their instrumentation.

With great glee Marc announced that he was adding such instruments as a Stylophone and a cheap children's organ, purchased in Woolworths, and he began his slow drift towards electrification. He realized the acoustic guitar and clay pots could not be sustained forever, and he still yearned to be a fully-fledged Jimi Hendrix style lead-guitarist. He sensed that he might alienate his loyal fans, just as Bob Dylan had caused outrage on his 1966 British tour by bringing an all electric rock band to back him, but as he began to play larger concert halls it made sense to seek louder amplification and a proper drum kit for Steve.

Up at his flat he checked out the possibilities of the electric guitar, and eventually used it on his summer of '69 single 'King Of The Rumbling Spires'. His love for Hendrix can be heard filtering through on the energetic and strangely effective self-taught guitar solos on the 1970 LP 'A Beard Of Stars', and in cuts like the remarkable 'Pavilions Of The Sun'. But even though Marc and Steve geared up the band for the group's first American tour of June 1969, the cosmic significance of these changes would be virtually meaningless as far as the American audiences were concerned. The tour was a great adventure for Marc, but was certainly not a success.

"What I adored about Marc was that he played every gig as if it was the one and only one," says June. "He was terribly good about getting there on time, and during the show he would give every fibre of his being. He would moan afterwards — about the sound if anything went wrong. But from the audience's point of view he gave absolutely everything. To him it was as vital as tomorrow."

June, Marc, Steve and a roadie called Ronnie flew out to New York for an inauspicious opening. They were due to play a small club on Bleeker Street the same night as the epoch making Woodstock Festival was being held.

While the super groups were flying in their tons of equipment to blast the eardrums of the Woodstock nation, Tyrannosaurus Rex turned up with all their gear in a station wagon. June mixed the sound on a desk with four levers.

They did their best to introduce the sparse crowd to the delights of 'The King Of The Rumbling Spires', and as Marc poured his soul into the songs and strummed with devout fury, he suddenly noticed his partner was acting in an increasingly strange fashion. Steve Peregrine Took rose unsteadily to his feet and began to take all his clothes off.

June: "Marc and I didn't know what was going on at the time, but we discovered later that Steve was dropping two tabs of acid a day. He took off all his clothes except for his underpants and began breaking up the equipment - we had so little to break anyway. We got back to the hotel and we just cried and cried. And we couldn't get rid of Steve - it was all just awful. He was a lousy bongo player and he went absolutely spare in America."

The last gig of the tour was at the Grand Ballroom, Seattle, and they were supporting a fine band called It's A Beautiful Day. For the first time Marc, the professional who was never late for a gig, vanished. He couldn't be found at the hotel, and June sent out search parties. No one had seen him all day. In desperation, June and the remnants of the Bolan entourage went to the ballroom.

"He arrived — out of his crust. He said he wouldn't go on, he was seeing monsters everywhere. But he went on and played incredibly loudly. The other band tried to talk him

down and make it a pleasant trip for him, and alleviate what was a dangerous situation. After that Steve just pissed off and left the band, and Marc and I came back to London. That's when we put an ad. in the *Melody Maker* for a gentle guy to play bongos."

In the event the replacement percussionist was recommended by June's friend John Lloyd. He was Mickey Finn, described to June as a painter. But she discovered that he was in fact a house painter who had worked on a mural for the Apple boutique, and also made a couple of records. 'He couldn't play congas particularly well, but he was beautiful. Mickey came round to the flat and played all day and I sat outside in the car while they got on with it."

Marc said to June later: "He can't sing. I don't know what to do. But he looks superb." Eventually, Michael Norman Finn joined Tyrannosaurus Rex and was pictured together with Marc for album covers and press.

Marc seemed none the worse for his bad LSD trip, and soon recovered his spirits after the disastrous American trip. He was determined to make sure all his fans knew he was alive and well and back in England. He was also worried that the image of Tyrannosaurus Rex might have taken a dent in Fleet Street, so one lunchtime he arrived unannounced at the *Melody Maker* office. Unfortunately, most of the staff were out at lunch, but for those who were left he staged an impromptu concert. He introduced Mickey Finn, the new replacement for Steve Took, a quiet bearded young man who silently obeyed Marc's every whim.

"This is Mickey — we've been really busy writing some new songs. Would you like to hear them?" Marc perched on a desk with his guitar, and Mickey beat time on desk tops and typewriters with his bare hands. Marc was clad in bright yellow satin trousers as if he were due on stage at the Roundhouse, and he threw back his head to sing a full selection from his next album. It was a wonderful performance that echoed through the building, but there was only one reporter and the office manager on hand to appreciate it. Within minutes there came a barrage of complaints and banging on the walls from the office of *Cycling* magazine next door. A year later, when Marc had become a superstar, a gang of girl fans burst into the same office hoping to steal the file of Bolan pictures from under the noses of the editorial staff. One of the girls caught sight of a reporter who bore a remarkable resemblance to Marc Bolan, and had the same mass corkscrew hair. The fans screamed and chased him down the corridor, thus saving the valuable file.

One important lesson had been learned from Marc's trip to America. He had to beef up the Tyrannosaurus Rex sound if it was to be a success beyond the confines of small clubs. While acoustic guitar was great for song-writing and jamming in his Toadstool studio, he really needed to develop his electric guitar playing. And who was the best guitarist around - the Master who could reveal his secrets to the eager pupil? Without hesitation, Marc chose Eric Clapton as his tutor, although the most famous guitarist in rock may not have realised he was being thus honoured.

Marc bought himself a Fender Stratocaster and set off to spend some time with Clapton at his Surrey home, where Blind Faith — the replacement group for Cream — was being put together. Marc just hung around and watched as Clapton, hailed as the greatest white blues guitarist, went through his paces. Nobody else would have had the cheek, but Bolan knew he needed more knowledge to put his plans for world domination into practice. The sorcerer's apprentice was about to try out some of his own magic.

Mickey Finn presented a wonderful contrast to Marc Bolan. Tall, bearded and quietly spoken, he loomed comfortably behind Marc, who was small and increasingly noisy. Thus when Mickey, without warning, shaved off his 'beard of stars' Bolan was furious and wouldn't speak to him for two days.

But the two went off to the seclusion of Wales to spend some time rehearsing and beefing up the sound of the band. Friends had urged Marc to add a bass guitar, but he had resisted the idea until Tony Visconti played some bass on the 1969 albums. Now that Steve Took had gone, Marc could go 'heavy'. He had to finish off 'A Beard Of Stars' virtually on his own, with Mickey overdubbing some Moroccan clay drums, backing vocals and finger cymbals. The album was released in March 1970 and was more 'electric' than anything he had dared to do before; and the music was much more rock influenced.

Marc had won another battle — to convince the world that Tyrannosaurus Rex had not broken up after its American trip. But work was hard to get, and the BBC rarely played his records on their conservative network. He could have allowed himself to become totally depressed, and others might have given up. But on January 30 Marc linked forces with his most powerful ally. He and June Child were married at Kensington Registry Office, a year-and-a-half after they first set up home together on Wimbledon Common.

It was a quiet wedding. A passer-by took a picture of the bride and groom with an instant camera, and it was later published in Disc, a weekly pop-paper. Steve Took was not among the guests at the impromptu pavement celebration.

June: "Steve came back from America weeks after us and nobody ever knew what had happened to him. But he wanted lots of money and Marc told him to bugger off. He kept 'phoning up and turning up at gigs. He thought he could leave and then just come back again. Later he joined the Pink Fairies and even they couldn't cope with him." From then on Steve went down a rocky road to oblivion and he died in 1980, choking to death on a cocktail cherry.

Marc was quite subtle in making the transition from acoustic to electric power. He'd use the Stratocaster for the last number at concerts, usually 'Elemental Child'. He was on particularly hot form the night of his concert at London's Queen Elizabeth Hall when he was supported by David Bowie, then introducing his mime act.

"Marc was a big draw in those days, before the records began to sell," says B.P. Fallon. 'I told him then he should get a bass guitar player, but at first he disagreed. Then when Tony Visconti played on his sessions, Marc decided to advertise for a bassist. All kinds of real dorks rang up."

Eventually Steve Currie from Hull turned up on his way to an audition for Manfred Mann's Chapter 3. Steve was nice, intelligent and played good bass. Marc was determined there should be no nonsense about him joining Manfred.

The new band began to take shape, and at last it adopted the shortened version of 'T.Rex', to help disc jockeys remember the name and ease their pronunciation problems. The ranks were swelled by the arrival of a real drummer, Bill Legent, and they had a consistent line-up in

time for the madness of Spring 1971.

"I don't claim to be a guitarist," said Marc. "But I've got flaming hands and bleeding fingers. I steer the guitar like a ship and sing with my eyes closed. When I'm bopping it feels great. I can't really beleive anybody can be called a pop star. No such thing. You might exist as one on a photograph, but it's never you."

The world waited breathless to see what Marc would do next. If he became a star, would it spoil him?

"If I get a hit — I'm changing my name to Zinc Alloy and I'll wear an aluminium suit."

Yet stardom seemed as elusive as ever. He kept putting out singles, and radio airplay was minimal. His January 1970 contender 'By The Light Of The Magical Moon' was almost totally ignored. One night he came stomping into the bar at the *Speakeasy*, a musician's haunt, now defunct, in London's Margaret Street. It was unusual for him to be there and he was in an impatient, angry mood. He didn't need encouraging to explain why. "I'm fed up with singles," he said. "It's hopeless in this country. I'll stick to albums from now on."

But Marc didn't give up singles, fortunately for his career. During the summer of 1970 he returned to his music room in the Notting Hill flat and began writing. The result, which he taped and played to June, was a remarkably catchy new song, with a loping beat and ear-grabbing hook-line. It was called 'Ride A White Swan'. He had written about swans before and the riff was somewhat similar to an earlier composition, but somehow the constituent parts came together to make up an obvious hit. The BBC *must* play this one, thought Marc. The time had come for T.Rex to supplant Tyrannosaurus, and for Marc to stand up and plug in the electric guitar.

After one play on the radio the record took off and began selling, and in November began its sensational rise up the charts. Marc's hour had come.

The record rose to number two in the chart, and in December he released the 'T.Rex' album, which also became a smash hit. Strings added by producer Tony Visconti had given an extra dimension to T.Rex music. Now there was no stopping the rise of what became dubbed 'T.Rextasy'.

Marc had lowered the price of tickets to all his concerts and as a result attracted a vast army of teenage girls who, almost overnight, swamped the older hippies and the student audience. Long-term fans who went to his show at the Lyceum, a large ballroom in the Strand, felt disappointed and disillusioned with the transformation. They were pleased that Marc had a hit after so many years, but could not take the screaming hysteria and Marc's projection as a rock star, dancing around on stage in a satin jacket and playing out of tune noisy lead guitar.

And yet — at a stroke — Marc had created a whole new mood for the Seventies. It was the dawning of the age of Glam-Rock. Gold lame and Elvis Presley-style posturing was revived for the first time in years.

The teenyboppers took over, demanding an end to woad, light shows, philosophizing and meditation. They wanted pure unadulterated pop music, and Marc Bolan gave it to them with joyous exultation. In his footsteps followed Slade, Gary Glitter, David Bowie, The Sweet, the Bay City Rollers and the Osmonds. They may not all have been directly influenced by him, but 'Ride A White Swan' and the beaming pop star splashed across the front pages of all the national newspapers and hogging all the TV and radio airtime, created the whole climate in which they could flourish.

When Marc put glitter under his eyes for a TV appearance his fans copied him, and his concerts turned into the sort of riot situations that had been a thing of the past. The phenomenon of the 'lookalike' fan began with Bolan and was later extended to Bowie and many other stars.

Marc was 24 years old, and life was now a gas. The nation's teenage girls fell for him just as their big sisters had fallen for Paul McCartney. but this time round the response was even wilder than it had been in Beatles days. Marc oozed sex appeal, and the girls at his concerts screamed and fainted in the aisles, rent their clothes and beat their chests. One concert in Boston, Lincolnshire in January 1972 caused such riots that there were 33 fainting cases who had to be treated for hysteria backstage. Boys as well as girls were affected.

A few months before the Boston show, when T.Rex played in Edinburgh, a youth of 17 had to be brought down with a flying tackle when he suddenly ran on stage and tried to grab Bolan. He was bundled off the side of the stage, and was later taken to his hero's dressing room where he shook hands with Marc. He confessed that he could not control his actions and had been driven wild by the excitement.

During the same tour, in November 1971, fans attacked eleven of the cars the group used to travel from gig to gig, and they had to be written off. Sometimes it took the promoter and his group nearly two hours to get away from the venues, such was the milling mob outside. It was terrifying — but it was fun.

Marc described it as "very unreal. A great strangeness. I've been doing what I always wanted to do, and finding out that it's altogether different from what one thought it would be. I come off stage sweating and wasted and people come up — very sweet people — and start asking me questions. It's tragic, there they are, the only time they've got to get near me, and I don't want to talk. They want to ask me how I got the name of the group. And all I'm thinking is how quickly we can get to the morotway cafe or if we've got any sandwiches."

Marc wasn't entirely convinced by his sudden rise as a pop idol, and still clung onto the idea of being accepted as a composer. "I'm not really sure why I'm doing this. I read a lot of people who say they are only in it for the money. I just don't know what they are talking about. surely, if money was the sole object you'd be a stockbroker. Money has brought me freedom, but it's brought a few bad times. I tend to obliterate bad times as soon as they've happened. It would be naive of me to say I didn't care about money, because money means freedom."

Marc seemed genuinely stunned by the overpowering pressures of his first year of stardom. The phones never stopped ringing, and he was in constant demand for interviews with every conceivable newspaper, magazine, radio and TV station. He found himself irritated by noise — the noise of fans, traffic, interviewers, managers, agents and even friends.

"Noise, I find, is more troublesome than it's ever been. I started off an introvers, and now I've had a six-month period of being an extrovert I think I'm slipping into the introvert bit again. It's very weird."

There was some comfort during this turmoil, like the knowledge that his hit 'Telegram Sam' had sold 200,000 copies in four days. "Now isn't that amazing?" said Marc. "It stuns me. I feel something incredible is happening and I am just a part of it. It's very painful for me to choose a new single because I am very aware of those two million people

out there. I saw 'Telegram Sam' as a trial. That was the first time I ever felt that way. I'm so easy to shoot down. All the rasping letters about me upset me for a week, or was it an hour? Well, I get over that sort of thing. I can become Zinc Alloy and say 'Go to hell babies, get off my back'. I can really say 'up yours' to anybody who says bad things. The only people who say bad things about me are jealous, vindictive people, and it really bugs them that I've got a white Rolls Royce. That's what bugs them, not the records. So I can be arrogant with those people.

"I'm lucky really that I'm not ahead of my time. I spent four years being ahead, but my time is *now*. I'm aware that I don't want to retreat. I know that. I'm prepared to fight. I like excitement, and that's why I wanted to be a teenage idol. But my head changes fast, and my habits change fast. I have to keep playing, otherwise I'd end up in a mental asylum."

How did fame affect Bolan? As money poured in and his power increased he threw off many of the constraints on behaviour society normally imposes. He couldn't help but gain satisfaction from the knowledge that those who once ignored him, or worse, made fun of his efforts, had egg on their face. The trouble was, he sometimes extended his bumptiousness to those who had supported him with great loyalty.

John Peel, who had driven Marc on gruelling jaunts up to Newcastle and back for £50 a night on their gigs together found that his old friend cooled towards him. He traced it back to an incident in early 1970 when Marc had sent him the acetate (test pressing) of 'By The Light Of The Magical Moon'. In all honesty, he didn't like it much and couldn't bring himself to play it on the radio. Marc was annoyed, and suddenly John found he was being frozen out. He called Marc several times, but Marc made excuses or just wasn't available. It seemed he didn't want to talk to him. After a few more calls Peel gave up trying to ring him. John preferred Marc when he hadn't been a star.

But he still cherished the memory of his old friend, and in particular the two pet hamsters that June and Marc had given him. When he set up his own record and publishing companies he named them after the hamsters - Dandelion and Biscuit.

Says June with regret: "Marc was surrounded by sycophantic people in the rock business, people who always said 'yes' to his ideas. He became a megalomaniac.

"Marc treated John like a minion, and John was incredibly hurt by it. He had given him his first chance on radio, but he never threw that fact at Marc. He had got him lots of gigs in the early days, and they were really close and adored each other. It was so silly and so sad that it could all be wiped out in one minute. The same thing happened with Tony Visconti. He was a very dear friend. Tony, Marc and I were like blood. Then Marc tried to put down Tony's contribution as a producer. He said: 'I don't need a producer. I can produce the records myself.' He became inflamed with his sense of importance and fame, and his God-given talent. He became impervious to anyone but himself."

It was almost as if Marc was terrified that anyone else might detract from his hard won success. He didn't want to share any credit or dilute his status. But it destroyed his relationship with Tony Visconti, who had stuck his neck out to help Marc break into the record industry. Hawk-like, Marc had watched Visconti at work on the recording desks, and decided he could do it all himself.

"It came to the point where you couldn't reason with him anymore. I was the only person to say 'no' to him," says

June. "He lost his sense of giving credit where it was due. The saddest thing of all was when he blew his relationship with Ringo Starr, who had been like a dad to him."

But there was a clue to this behaviour which soon became apparent. His condition was exacerbated by a new development in Marc's private life. In common with many rock stars of the period he was introduced to the habit of sniffing cocaine. It became common practice in the music press to complain that many musicians seemed to have developed swollen heads. 'Ego-tripping' was the phrase, and the cause in most cases was cocaine damaging the personality, increasing hostility and suspicion to the point of paranoia.

"If you do a volume of cocaine it makes you drink more," says June, "and you drink without getting drunk. It alters your character completely, and you can't see the wood for the trees."

Marc was turned onto coke in New York while making his 'Electric Warrior' album. He rang June to own up. She became increasingly tired of his outbursts of temper and fantasising. Once Marc asked her opinion on some music and she responded that she honestly thought it was rubbish. He replied by throwing a magnum of champagne at her head. She ducked just in time and the bottle smashed into a partition wall where it stuck with the neck protruding. She went out into the hall without a word and came back with an empty picture frame which she placed around the champagne bottle. "It was a reminder," she says.

Even more pressure was put on their marriage by the constant attention of fans. Marc was idolised, and couldn't go out into the streets without being mobbed. Nothing had happened like it in England since Beatle days.

The couple moved from Notting Hill at last to a more palatial house in Clarendon Gardens. 1971 was a long hot summer, and yet it was impossible for them to go and enjoy themselves unmolested. They spent most of the summer hiding inside the house with the curtains drawn. Even when they moved to Bilton Tower in Great Cumberland Place, where there was security and an underground carpark, fans would hail a taxi to try and get past the porters and up into their flat.

"We had to crawl about on our hands and knees to avoid being seen during the day, and we could hardly go out at night except to Tramp, the night club."

Marc and June had been in the habit of going to visit Guy the Gorilla, a huge and popular beast incarcerated in Regent's Park Zoo. They regularly brought him cauliflower and swore that he recognised them. At least Guy didn't ask Marc for his autograph. Bolan had become so famous they couldn't even go shopping, and everything had to be ferried into their home. But early one morning they decided they would risk a trip to see Guy.

They arrived at the zoo at around 10 am, and only the animals and keepers were about. Otherwise there was not a soul to be seen. Suddenly June spotted a girl in a school uniform. Under her breath June muttered "Don't look, just walk slowly away." But Marc turned round before she could stop him and the girl let out a yell: "That's Marc Bolan!"

She was with a party of fifty school girls who had just arrived and they went berserk. "They were after us like the Hound of the Baskervilles," says June. The girls screamed and Marc and June ran, quaking with fear across the park. "We couldn't hide in Guy's cage. He was forty then, and he was a very delicate eater. He was our favourite, but we couldn't go and see him anymore."

Marc needed a bodyguard, and in future he had one whenever he went on expeditions, even to the pub to meet journalists. June tried to keep herself well hidden, ducked out of photo sessions with Marc and avoided all interviews.

Marc may once have believed that stars "didn't exist", but they did in the hearts and minds of the young girls who bombarded him with gifts and fan mail. "It was monumental," said June. "We couldn't even put our rubbish out. We had to put it in the boot of the car and drive it to a friend's dustbin. We called it the rubbish run. It took me ages to work out what was happening. We would find all this rubbish on the steps and then realised it was ours. The fans had been rooting through our dustbin for souvenirs."

Once a young girl turned up outside their door with bleeding feet. She had hitch-hiked from Scotland to see Marc. They put plasters on her feet, gave her some money and told her to go home. Later the police called, trying to trace the missing child.

The days of the old van were over for the Bolans. They now owned a beautiful white 1957 Rolls Royce which bore them round town and to gigs. Only June was allowed to drive. "I loved that car. It was a real status symbol. It was so ironic that Marc should die in a car crash, because he never drove."

There was one occasion when Marc decided he should learn to drive. They had motored in a Mini down to a friend's house in East Grinstead. In a quiet country lane June gave Marc his one and only lesson. She talked him through the clutch and brake pedal routine, and the car moved off at 4 mph.

"Stop it!" yelled Marc in great panic. "I want to get out!" He felt he had no control over the car's movements and the mechanical beast seemed completely alien.

"He hated it, and he hated other people driving as well," says June. "He was afraid of dying. He once told my mother that he wouldn't live beyond 30. And of course he died two weeks before his thirtieth birthday. My mum told me what he had said to her, two weeks after the funeral."

June was at Marc's side throughout his period of greatest success. They had been immensely happy, but their life was becoming a hell for them both. Marc wanted his freedom, and June was tired of trying to constrain him.

Friends recall the night when Marc was at the Speakeasy, somewhat inebriated and skulking in the restaurant. The club's telephone rang; it was June: "Where is he?" "Don't tell June I'm here!" implored the renegade husband.

Most of the rock fraternity spent the early part of the Seventies in an advanced state of intoxication anyway, so Marc was not alone. Photographer Barrie Wentzell recalled the night he was given a lift by Marc and June in the white Rolls Royce back to London after a provincial gig on a T.Rex tour. "We stopped on the way for the call of nature," recalls Barrie. "June stopped the car right by a ditch and I jumped out straight into a huge puddle. When I got back in I was covering the seats with mud which was all over me, while at the same time Marc was leaning out of the other window being sick, and of course the brandy was damaging the paintwork. June was furious with both of us."

But the split, when it came, was not just due to a few minor rows and escapades. "It was other women", she says. "He wasn't promiscuous, but he always had to fall in love with them. After his third affair I didn't want it anymore, and that was when Gloria Jones came along. The funny thing was - I introduced them to each other."

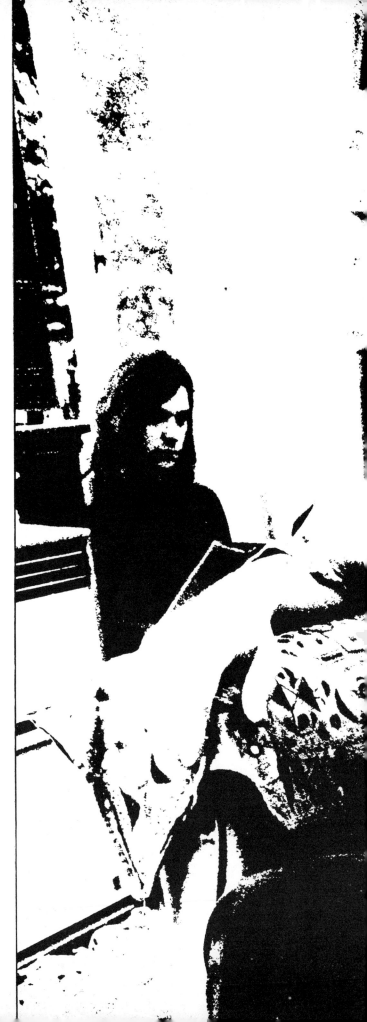

The Bopping Imp had changed overnight into the Metal Guru. He was the Prettiest Star and Zinc Alloy, an over-powering combination of charm and egotism. Just as he was upsetting his friends in private, so his public image began to be tarnished by his increasingly strident claims and comments.

The British public are quick to give acclaim but equally swift to condemn any hint of the vice they detest most of all. They can forgive a whiff of sexual ambivalence, even applaud it, and they will tolerate high-living and self-indulgence. But they cannot stand a big head. And unfortunately, for the opening months of the new decade, Marc seemed to suffer from the biggest attack of swollen cranium in showbusiness.

He began to appear outrageously camp where once he had been soft, shy and fey. The introvert had become extrovert with a vengeance, and he began to incur the growing hostility of critics and reporters who, as detached observers, owed him no particular allegiance. An edition of BBC TV's early-evening show *Nationwide* featured a whole selection of Bolan hits in quick succession and

pointed out how they all sounded the same. It was unfair, but Bolan was beginning to set himself up for ridicule.

The influential *New Musical Express* concluded one less than enraptured article on him with the author's comment: "I didn't like him very much." The praise turned faint, and then vanished.

His pronouncements had become harsher. Marc was a tremendously entertaining conversationalist - most of the time his flow of words and ideas were more important to him than the actual deeds. He was under no illusions that rock'n'roll as a subject was very boring, particularly when it came to calculating album sales in South America or the cost of transporting equipment to the Floral Hall, Southport. In the old days he would much sooner talk about magic.

This was typical of the stream of ideas he would pour out in interviews: "I believe elves existed. Not as elves, but as strong, wise people, like the Atlanteans. People will mock of course, but they are only capable of violent emotion, which is easy. But it's harder to feel tender and affectionate to others. I believe in the magic of life. The Earth is a house for us to live in, but people put up fences and pay bits of silver and say: 'This bit is mine - get out.' The elf people have died out or walked off the earth into a rainbow. Only the people who wear metal underwear and have black blood are left."

During such flights of fancy it was impossible not to be entranced by Marc as he wished himself into a nirvana like state. B.P. Fallon remembers a night when he and Marc were stopped from drinking in the BBC Club at the *'Top Of The Pops'* studios. They had to sit in the corridor between takes. Marc said: "What do they expect us to do - drink dew drops out of rose petals?"

But there came a time when you couldn't talk to Marc - he talked at you. The words poured out, sometimes funny, sometimes boastful, often with a harder, more practical edge. "We've got to hype these people in the business, so we can get money and standing to do our next thing. I never regarded commercialism as important. But when one play of 'Ride A White Swan' on Radio One sent 20,000 out to buy it in London alone, that speaks for itself." However, Bolan was not impervious to criticism: "When all those letters came in saying all my hits sound the same, I was really hurt. The more that success is given to you, if you have any lasting qualities as an artist, the more humble you become."

Humility had not been his most obvious characteristic when T.Rex soared to fresh heights in the exciting months that followed the breakthrough with 'Ride A White Swan.' The hits came thick and fast. In 1971 he scored with 'Hot Love', 'Get It On' and 'Jeepster'. In the following twelve months came 'Telegram Sam', 'Metal Guru', 'The Children Of The Revolution', and 'Solid Gold Easy Action', the latter coupled with 'Born To Boogie'.

The titles were slick, the words usually meaningless, and the beat increasingly urgent. But his best work of the period was the album 'Electric Warrior', which also boasted one of the simplest and most effective album covers of all time. It pictured Marc in dark silhouette outlined in gold, clutching his guitar in front of a stack of amplifiers.

At that time Marc was still teamed with Mickey Finn, but had added vocal power from Howard Kaylan and Mark Volman, two Americans who had once been part of the Sixties group the Turtles, and who later teamed up with Frank Zappa. They met Marc on his first American tour and found they all enjoyed the same sense of humour.

They sang back-up vocals on 'Hot Love' and 'Get It On', and the latter track was number one for four weeks, a fact which the ex-Turtles never tired of pointing out. Apparently they joined the ranks of those who felt miffed at Marc's lapses of courtesy.

He was now in a position to sort out his place in the 'industry of human happiness'. He quit the Fly Record label to sign a deal with EMI, and set up his own T.Rex label, together with his own Wizard publishing company. The hours spent song writing in the cold water flat had repaid him with pure gold.

'Get It On' was re-titled with the second line of the song, 'Bang A Gong' for American consumption, and it proved to be the big hit he was waiting for in the States. Marc felt like he was flying as he thrilled to the acclaim of a concert at the prestigious Carnegie Hall in New York City. It was a long way from helping on his mum's barrow in Berwick Street market. And there were more thrills to come.

In March 1972 he played two concerts at the Empire Pool, Wembley, that were complete sell-outs, and there were scenes of utter hysteria. Marc had developed a friendship with ex-Beatles drummmer Ringo Starr, and they made a film together of the concert, filled out with improvised clips of Marc clowning and giggling. It was released as 'Born To Boogie' at the end of the year and was a big box-office success in Britain. He had three albums released that year, his official one for EMI, 'The Slider', and two re-issues on Fly - 'Bolan Boogie', and a double LP release featuring his old Tyrannosaurus Rex material.

In 1973 Marc released a rather predictable album called 'Tanx' which had the star on the cover dressed in a kind of feather boa and exposing his chest, whilst crouched over a large model tank with projecting gun barrel. It included such cuts as 'Life Is Strange' and 'Electric Slim & The Factory Hen', but the mixture was as before, and the sharpness of 'Electric Warrior' was missing. Tracks like 'Rapids' were relatively sloppy.

His single releases that year were 'Twentieth Century Boy', 'The Groover' and 'Truck On Tyke' and were mostly attempts to recapture the magic of 1971-2 that was already beginning to fade. The critics were beginning to say he was finished.

But he wasn't going to let go that easily after battling for recognition, and when America seemed to find it hard to take his music, he toured there all the more. It was in L.A. in 1973 that he met Gloria Jones.

Gloria was a producer as well as a singer and songwriter. She joined Marc's band on the road as a back-up vocalist together with Pat Hall. Gloria sang with Marc on his 'Truck On Tyke' single, but it didn't achieve a very high chart-placing and it began to look like Marc was going to fade away with the Glam-Rock movement.

Watching his progress and then his decline from afar was June Bolan. They never became divorced and today she describes herself as 'the widow Bolan'. They obtained a decree nisi, but says June: "Neither Marc nor I wanted a decree absolute. We couldn't make that final severance. We went through two years of absolute hell when there was no communication between us. I last saw him three months before his death, at a charity lunch for Music Therapy. I was to receive a prize and I knew Marc would be there. I went on stage to collect the prize and he was sitting at the top table, next to Gary Glitter."

Marc asked June to come and see him in his limousine and invited her to spend the afternoon with him. "He wanted someone to talk to." It was a traumatic meeting. June cried as Marc told her: "If you hadn't left, none of this

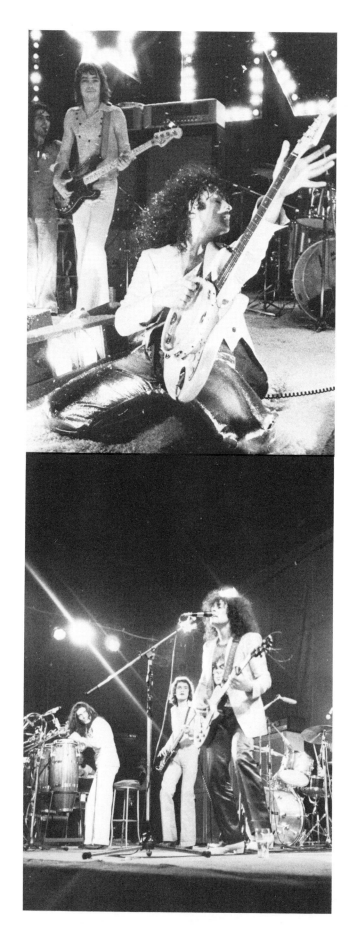

would have happened." But it was too late for a reunion, and they never saw each other again.

Marc had found new happiness with Gloria Jones, and in 1975 the couple had a child, Roland Seymour, who they called Rolan Bolan. The union between Marc and Gloria provided Bolan with considerable stability, which he needed after enduring the ravages of the pop lifestyle.

For a year he lived in a hotel in France and drank brandy, with serious consequences for his once perfect looks. "He locked himself away when he got fat," says June. "He was always so proud of his body, and now he hated the way he looked. He only went out at night, to clubs where people would accept him. He wasn't happy living in hotels. Librans need homes. When I left him he never had a proper house for a long time. It was just a few months before his death that he bought a house in Sheen."

During his period of heavy drinking Marc began to show signs of paranoia, and his personality underwent further changes. It reached the point where one of his best and most influential friends had to ask him to leave his house after a particularly bad scene. His music became increasingly like a parody of his old self, and reached a new low with the clumsily titled 'Zinc Alloy And The Hidden Riders Of Tomorrow Or A Creamed Cage In August' album. He sang with customary vigour, sounding like early Bob Dylan on the driving 'Venus Loon', complete with funky backing vocals and a blasting Pop Arts Orchestra. Gloria, her brother Richard and Pat Hall were the back-up singers, but it was all an attempt to gain credibility in America. British fans listened with increasing indifference.

"Before, he only did things he liked," says June. "He never constructed records for the market. When he tried to make records for America they lacked his intuitive thing, and then he became desperate. He made some awful records, that were so empty and lacked all his wonderful warmth and feeling. The music has a frantic quality."

Marc came back to England and virtually abandoned his attempts to crack America. He toured all round the world, then his drummer Bill left and T.Rex was due for a major shake up. In 1974 he joked about his own slipping fame by releasing a single called 'Whatever Happened To The Teenage Dream', and he set off on a British tour with Gloria and a revamped T.Rex. 'Teenage Dream' was an unusual ballad for Marc, with lots of sliding strings,and fine soul vocal support from Gloria. It was a lot better than 'Light Of Love' and 'Zip Gun Boogie', his other single releases of the year, both dispiriting flops.

When the decline came it seemed all the more painful for Marc's admirers because it became so prolonged and unnecessary. It was believed he had suffered a mild heart-attack during his darkest days, and the shock to his system may well have helped restore his sanity and his iron resolve. By 1973, Marc was rounder in the face, but saner.

And for a man who was supposed to be slipping in popularity, he remained remarkably cool and cheerful. He admitted he had gone over the top in his behaviour and attitude towards people, and called that era 'The Madness'. He even indicated a certain self-dislike for his own extravagant posturing. About his 1971 self he said: "I didn't like *her* at all." He felt he had more freedom to experiment in his music, which showed that he wasn't entirely concerned with getting endless hits. "I'd like to do an LP of poetry, or electronic music. I've got my own label to do it on, without harming the validity of T.Rex. All this doesn't mean I'll put out 55 LPs of me farting in the moonlight, but it will free me from instant comparisons.

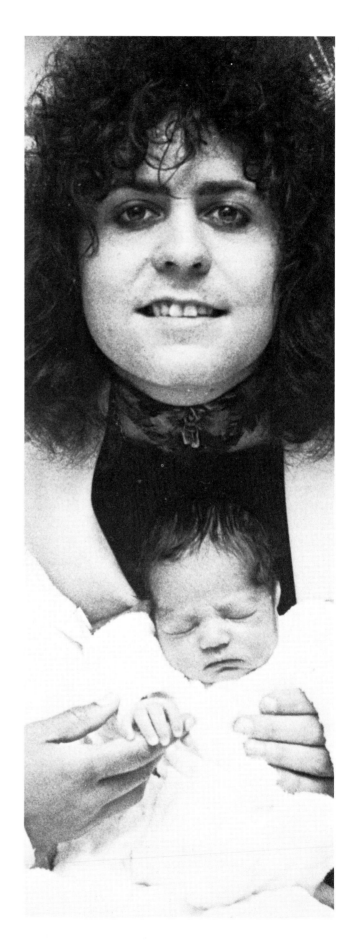

And if I'm not well established now, I never will be."

Marc pointed out he had appeared 'laidback' for a year, keeping a low profile, and all the other cover-ups for non-headline status. "That was deliberate," he insisted. "I was allowing the madness to move away. I enjoyed the madness and being born to boogie, but I can see more clearly now. I'll accept that I'm blatantly commercial 'cos I enjoy it. But I'd like to do something beyond the simple Bolan rock'n'roll, and if only a quarter of the kids come with it, then it wouldn't matter."

Marc was being deadly serious, and gone was his talk of elves, dwarves and metal underwear. He wanted growth, development and above all, one sensed, the respect of other musicians. "I don't want to go on the road now for fear of being involved in the dying embers of Glam Rock. I don't feel involved in it - even if I started it. That's not my department anymore. I found Glam Rock embarrassing, personally, and not what I really wanted to do. I'm not quite convinced that a performer has to be a freak. I'm just a street punk."

Marc's use of the latter phrase was particularly interesting, coming some three years before the arrival of punk rock. He explained that he felt he 'moved away' from T.Rextasy at the right moment, neatly turning around the argument that perhaps it had moved away from him. "I enjoyed being screamed at initially. When it started it was a phenomenon. Chicks were screaming and pulling my hair out. But now that sort of thing is commonplace, and it's lost the whole point of what it was all about. After a while the phenomenon loses its originality - totally. I enjoyed it, sure, and the whole thing was lovely, if you can look at it with humour. I want to avoid resting on my laurels. I feel obliged to the kids and to the industry to do something in return. Rock'n'roll is a great thing, and it still gets me off, and there are a million things I still want to do."

Marc was, like many rock musicians conscious of their position, prone to announce the existence of grandiose schemes that somehow never materialised. He'd get an idea that would help expand the frontiers of his achievements, hold discussions, release titbits of information to the press, but never actually put his ideas into conception. He planned animated cartoons, full-length films, and a pop opera. There was a science fiction movie proposed called 'Cosmic Messiah' but it was never made. Nor was a film with David Niven.

Marc revealed in 1973 that he was planning a T.Rex documentary. "I've got so much footage we could use, covering the rise of T.Rex. I did a really good film for *Top Of The Pops* too, which was Glam-Rock at its peak! But later on I'd like to take an acting role that had nothing to do with being Marc Bolan. I did quite a bit of acting as a kid. Ringo is such a good actor, but he won't admit it. I might do a TV series for Japan and call myself 'Zinc Alloy' for the part."

Even if Bolan never became a film actor, at least he could boast a success at the movie houses in his singing role. It must have reminded him of his old favourite Al Jolson, who had revolutionised the cinema with the first talkie *The Jazz Singer*.

"'Born To Boogie' was dynamite," said Marc. "There was a lot wrong with it, but it was made as a lightweight piece of T.Rex propaganda. Everytime the school holidays are on we put it out. What's that great American phrase? 'A film for the youth market'. You know, I'm just surprised I survived. I got heavily overexposed, and I had to make a controlled move to hold back on everything. In three years I had ten hits. I'm just surprised that I'm here at all. I still can't walk down the street without getting stopped."

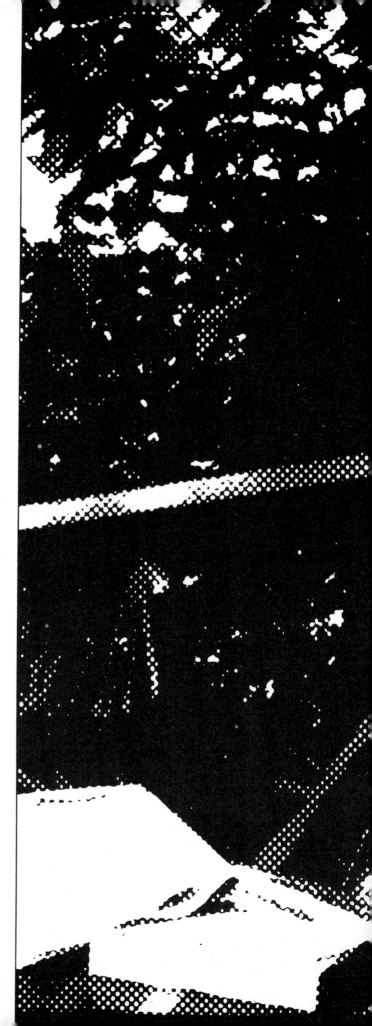

The Madness had gone. The teenage dream had faded, and Marc had known troughs of despair that were only shared by his closest friends and associates.

The public, largely ignorant of Bolan's mental anguish, saw only that the hitmaker had lost his magic touch. He had suffered a nervous breakdown while young, a minor heart attack, and endured the debilitation of drug and alcohol abuse and a broken romance. It says much for Marc's strength of character and will power that he overcame all these setbacks without begging for public sympathy and always managed to win through.

Throughout it all he kept up his bubbling good spirits, and would bounce back from any fit of gloom or depression. In January 1974, Marc and T.Rex toured England again. The band were rocking, and Marc whipped up the audience to fever pitch once more.

Backstage the band sometimes welcomed visitors, and there wasn't the great security blackout that so often surrounds the more paranoid and suspicious rock touring-parties. The band then consisted of Steve Currie and Mickey Finn, with Pat Hall and Gloria Jones supplying the vocals. It was Marc's first tour in two years, and he was happy to be back on the road, even if he was disguising himself as 'Zinc Alloy'.

But the rest of the year was not so much fun for Marc. He broke up with June as his affair with Gloria grew more important, and even his old pal Mickey Finn left the band to get completely out of the music business. Marc's album 'A Creamed Cage In August' was a flop, and the following year his 'Zip Gun Boogie' single and album were both panned and barely charted. This was his darkest hour.

Characteristically, within a year he was back and clamouring for attention. One of his first acts was to produce a good single, 'New York City' which was a hit for him in summer 1975, and shortly after that he began a series of interview spots with various celebrities on ITV's *Today* programme. Among those he interviewed was Keith

Moon, who attempted to send Marc up, which was Moon-the-cruel as opposed to Moon-the-loon. Among those watching was June Bolan, who found herself cringing with embarrassment. "I was mesmerised, like a mongoose by a snake. I hated every second of it, and really thought he shouldn't have been doing it. I just couldn't believe it."

But if Marc was not as good an interviewer as the producers had hoped, he was on top form on Mike Mansfield's *Supersonic*, the London Weekend TV show that was producing some of the best telly pop since *Ready Steady Go!* Mansfield was a great supporter of the Bolan talent, and regularly used him on the show, which was recorded each week at the ITV company's South Bank studios. The graffiti scrawled by hysterical fans still remains on the walls of adjacent buildings.

At one show in October 1975, Marc was to sing his new single 'Dreamy Lady'. The week before on the same show he'd been drenched in foam, smoke and bubbles as he sang. This time he was to rise from the floor while a pneumatic star on which he lay raised him up and flashed its myriad light bulbs, with musical accompaniment from his new band. On the same bill were Sweet and David Essex, but as usual the Bolan magic drew all eyes to him. In an interview before the show he drew outrageous comparisons with himself and super-fast guitarist John McLaughlin, and philosophised, joked and let forth a stream of ideas. As he built up verbal speed, Gloria Jones sat by listening with round eyes, obviously fascinated by Marc in full flight.

And yet there was the other side to Marc, detectable beneath the flash and showmanship. Quiet, patient, waiting his turn for the cameras, buying drinks for his band or sitting chatting to his producer, relaxed, attentive, charming. He talked about plans to tour once more in 1976, and of the bad times that had dogged his recent career. But first he talked about the joys of parenthood. It transpired that Marc had been present at the delivery, and even that had turned into a Bolan epic.

"Yeah - I delivered the baby myself", smiled Marc. "I was a bit nervous about it, but it just sort of popped out! In a way it was an anticlimax, because it was a week late. I was doing my first *Supersonic* recording session, and I had a call to say Gloria was in labour. I went home and got caught in the rush hour, and then by the time I got to the hospital it had already started. The baby let out a few yells and suddenly there was this big soul voice - 'Oh, yeah!' " Marc and Gloria both dissolved with laughter at this dramatisation of events. "Man, it was great. Now I'm a midwife," said Marc. "No - it's great having a kid. It's changed my whole life. You see, I don't feel like I'm a father, I feel like his brother, 'cos you know, I'm not a dad type. I never think about dads. My mum was my person, the one I related to, and I've always loved her."

Rolan was the same star sign as Marc, and was born four days before his father's birthday. Marc then made a rather curious comment: "I had his horoscope read and it's exactly the same as mine. Scarey? My birthday is the 30th September, and he came on the 26th. It has changed me a lot. It gets very empty being a rock star. I was beginning to feel very unfulfilled over the last year or so, even though there was the relationship with Gloria and I love her very much."

Marc explained that he wasn't about to start a Bolan dynasty, but he wanted someone to teach and to learn from. "You can learn a lot from kids. They come out so pure. And we're soiled. We are soiled goods." It was a brilliant phrase, and he said it with serious concern. "The

day I found out there was a baby due I was scared of it, because of a responsibility I'd never had before. Business I can handle. Rock'n'roll - easy, you can normally do something about that. But this poor little tyke, well, I'm going to be totally responsible." Although Marc was genuine in his feelings for his young son, in the same breath he admitted that the baby was then in the hands of a nurse. "But it's the first time Gloria has left him. I'd bring him here, but it's too early. Later on he'll go everywhere with me."

Marc thought that the kids of famous rock parents would probably grow up and take over the rock business and cited Zowie Bowie and Keith Richard's Marlon. "Rod Stewart will probably have kids...they'll grow up and take over."

Marc did not think that being a father would interfere with his career, indeed he considered it would be a great help. "With any artist you have ups and downs, and that's often because there is no motivation. The initial motive is - 'I wanna be a star'. And then you become a star and nobody actually tells you what happens after you become famous, about how you get crucified 95 times a week. You don't realise what's happening to you at first, because you're on the road all the time, and having six number one hits. For two years I've been off the road and had time to reflect and think about what I'm doing. It gets disconcerting. A lot of things I did, I could have done better."

Marc said he felt like Bob Dylan had beforehis motorcycle accident. Bob had been on an Australian tour and one night found himself sitting at a typewriter, and suddenly had no idea why he was typing and felt scared, as if thousands of invisible people were pushing him against a wall.

Marc: "When you've got deadlines everyday, not just for gigs, but so many things, well - booze and drugs don't help. That wasn't my problem. My problem was loneliness. That's why my marriage broke up. When I met Gloria it solved my problem of loneliness, because she can really live with a musician. You can cook with someone like that, and also, she is a better singer than me! Gloria has had hit records. She's done it all. It was a big chance for me to be with someone like that and I didn't feel lonely, and didn't feel the need to put on a facade. But I'm still going through changes. The changes don't stop. The difference is how I handle them. I put my head through a brick wall once. I didn't throw TVs out of windows, but I used to smash mirrors all the time. I was ultra violent."

Marc had been known to beat up girlfriends, but the one episode that really upset him did not involve women, but a guitar. "It was my first Les Paul Gibson and I smashed it up. It was just after 'Hot Love' and I'd done a disastrous tour of America. I had no reason to go there in the first place. I'd only been playing electric guitar for about four weeks and I was off to America playing on the same bills as Mountain and the Grateful Dead. I mean - COME ON! They really needed me - right? What saved me was still being number one when I came back to England because it was up there for nine weeks. But in America I grew so dejected and I threw that Les Paul across the stage, and as I watched it go through the air I thought: 'You can't do that to a delicate instrument'. And the neck went."

Marc made an expressive noise of a valuable guitar snapping. "I'd broken the most precious thing I had. It was unnecessary, and it was just punishing myself. It was due to total frustration. But here I am six years later and I'm still happening. Check it out. I did four ballroom gigs a few

94

months ago with no promotion, just to see how things were.
I wondered if they would just sit there and look at me. I
didn't know. The gigs sold out and the response was
amazing - with no publicity. The local kids turned out and
it went down well. But it could have bombed - and we
wanted to bomb in secret! There was no way I was going to
do nine days at the Royal Albert Hall. I had no theatrics,
just a five piece band."

Marc announced that he had recorded four albums,
including one with Gloria and one with her brother. "Her
brother, no, not my brother. Harry - yes, he's still driving
buses, bless him. But boy, have I been working!" Although
Marc hated and resented being written off by the
unsympathetic, he was much more willing to admit past
failures, now that he was past the first flush and conceits of
youth.

"There was a definite period when it wasn't happening.
It all got to be a damp squib. I'd become a money-making
machine and that was very obvious, and I was putting my
impetus into things other than T.Rex. I wasn't sure if I
wanted T.Rex to continue. But now I want the deejays to
say 'T.Rex', because I want to include the boys as a group.
There was a lot of confusion with Mickey Finn leaving. He
was a partner right at the beginning, but towards the end
the musicianship I wanted changed." Marc was very good
at placing himself in the league tables of stardom, and
would have made an excellent rock journalist. He already
had most of the qualifications. He couldn't spell and had
atrocious handwriting. But in 1975, he wasn't planning on
giving up music right away. "I always think most pop stars
last for five years, and I'm into my sixth, which means I'll be
okay for another ten. I've had my lean period. Last year
was very bad for me. It was a bad year for all Librans. The
records I made were very below par. They were 'run-out'
energywise. And so were Lennon's, and he's another
Libran."

Marc talked excitedly about his next album, which was
'Futuristic Dragon', on which he said he'd spent a hundred
thousand pounds. He'd even recorded his follow up album
to that, and said he'd got back his old production speed.
He snapped his fingers furiously like a New York lawyer
outlining his case against the Federal Government.

"After 'Tanx' the band was stale; but there was a product
commitment...I had to release two albums a year and five
singles. I didn't really want to play on 'Zinc Alloy', which
was very patchy." He worked on an album with Pat Hall for
six months, edited his movie 'Born To Boogie' for
American release, and experimented with video. "I even
took acting and tap dancing lessons for a while, and played
a lot of guitar with friends in L.A. Gloria introduced me to a
whole different breed of musician."

Where had Marc been living for the past few years? "All
over the place". Could Gloria keep up with him? "So far".
Didn't he ever feel like putting down roots in one place?
"Yes I do. Have to, now we've got a kid. I'm looking for a
house in England, somewhere not too far from town, like
Kingston. I don't want to get it together in the country. But I
am going to keep my house in L.A., which Bowie is living in
at the moment." Was it a mansion? "Oh well, there's a
swimming pool and eight bedrooms. You know me, I don't
live cheap." He snapped his fingers a few more times.
Everyone laughed. "Monte Carlo? That was the first place I
got shipped to when I was a tax exile. It was great for about
four weeks. I made a big mistake in buying a big
penthouse and shipping all my gear out there. I was there
for four months with no friends, nothing to stimulate me. I
nearly went crazy and became a cognac freak and put on

about two stone through eating."

Was getting fat a sign of contentment?

"Contentment? No man, it was a sign of being drunk. I was going mad with boredom. But looking back, even at the lowest ebb of my career, it would be a high for most people, and I realised that I was taking too much for granted. When you only get to 25 in the chart with a record, that is not the end of the world. When I got to 28 with 'Debora', I was knocked out. So now I'm just pleased to have the chance to make records at all. I've had six straight number ones, and maybe more, and four number twos — doesn't this sound terrible? It's like *Performance*, when James Fox as Turner says Mick Jagger was 'never that big' and a little girl says: 'well, he's had one number one, two two's and a number three'. I've only ever had one real flop and that was 'Zip Gun Boogie'. Nobody pounced on me, because they had been predicting my downfall for so long. I remember playing Colston Hall, Bristol just before 'White Swan' broke, and a guy wrote 'This is the first nail in Bolan's coffin'. I had kicked Mickey Finn or something because he had a bad hand and couldn't play, and I called him a silly cunt on stage. 'You silly cunt', I said, 'You silly cunt'. And the week after we were in the Top Ten. My coffin must have a lot of fucking nails. But I don't feel victimised any more, because it happens to everyone. What matters to me are my friends, and other musicians."

What about his new role as TV interviewer? Apart from Keith Moon, his other guests had included John Mayall, the blues-band leader, and he'd even chatted up Telly Savalas, then making waves as Kojak. He regarded the whole exercise as a lot of fun, despite the recalcitrance of Keith Moon. "It's been good for me after my laid back period. I want to do Gary Glitter next. They can't bullshit me, because I'm the biggest bullshitter of all time. And I don't want to be the star of the show. They are the stars, talking to the public about their problems, and I can relate to them from experience. And they won't necessarily be music business people. I'll be talking to Stan Lee of Marvel Comics. Anyone who invented Spiderman has got to be interesting."

Marc said he'd been offered late night chat shows, but he wanted to stay a rock'n'roller, doing what he did best. He most wanted T.Rex to sound like it should have done four years earlier - and hadn't. "The time has now come where I don't give a monkey's and I shall just do what I want. I'd like to get Margaret Thatcher on TV and interview her. I want to link rock'n'roll with what's going on in the world - like drug problems and violence. They are the realities. What are the realities of rock'n'roll? All the money - it's only paper. All the cars have been written off. All the guitars have been smashed. The dream has gone. And now it's a huge medium, an audio visual art, from 'Tommy' to...whatever." Wasn't he supposed to be playing a psychotic murderer in a big budget movie. What happened to that particular dream?

"I'm still signed for it but they couldn't get the money up. They were only a million short. But it's a great script. It'll get done, but it's far more important for me to be back on the map musically." Bolan was back and firing on all cylinders.

Mike Mansfield, the TV director, did a great deal to help Marc during this transition period, and gave him considerable freedom and scope to make his appearances on *Supersonic* as effective and dramatic as possible. They had first met when Mike was producing a pop quiz show for Southern TV, presented by Muriel Young, another producer who was to help Marc in his last year. "We used

Marc quite a lot on the quiz show," says Mike. "He was a
regular member of the panel, along with Paul Jones,
Marianne Faithfull, Sandie Shaw and Justin Hayward.
Marc was very good and knew all the answers. This was in
the late 'Sixties, just before 'Ride A White Swan' took off."

Mike was able to renew his friendship with Marc when
T.Rex performed 'Telegram Sam' on the Russell Harty
Show, which he produced. Mansfield: "When I launched
Supersonic there were two people who were perfect
material for the show, Gary Glitter and Marc Bolan. And
Marc put tremendous creative input into the show. He was
rather similar to Adam Ant - both of them very creative
people." Artists were given extraordinary freedom, and the
cameras had free rein to work 'in the round', which meant
they darted all over the studio. Marc Bolan looked like he
lived in the studio and loved every minute of it, Mansfield
remembers. "Marc was so enthusiastic and inventive.
When he did 'Ride A White Swan' we built an enormous
swan which ran on a pneumatic truck, and he was to ride it
like a charioteer, trundling around the studio while we
dropped barrow loads of goose feathers from the gantry
overhead. Two things went wrong," says Mike. "The truck
broke down half way round and Marc had to sing with his
back to the audience - and he laughed his head off. Then
two days later, they were recording an edition of *Upstairs,
Downstairs* in the same studio and you know what
happened, of course. Goose feathers began falling during
the entire day's shoot." One of the problems with Marc was
the suggestiveness of his performances on the show,
which Mike gently tried to discourage. One of these was
when Marc sang the old number 'I Ain't Going Nowhere'
with Gloria Jones. She was in skintight lurex and draped in
barrage balloon material. Then one of the stage hands
decided he wanted to join in. He went to the wardrobe
department and returned dressed like the man of mystery
in the Sandeman Port advertisements. "He chose to put a
foam machine between his legs and covered Gloria in
foam while she was singing, and of course it was very
suggestive," says Mike. The show was sponsored by the
US Army for American screening, and they wouldn't
accept it. They feared it might adversely affect their
recruitment drive.

Marc also joined in these sexy antics, and sometimes
had to be warned off of gyrating his hands and hips in such
a fashion as would cause outrage in Mrs. Whitehouse
country. But it was all tremendous fun, and between takes,
while drinking in the bar, Marc would outline his plans for a
futuristic TV show that would feature himself and mime
artists like Marcel Marceau and Lindsay Kemp. If David
Bowie could do it, why not his little buddy Marc?

"He had great ideas for presentation" says Mike. "Like
the giant star, which he also used on tour. Once we flew
him on wires across the studio and he wanted to fly out
over the audience. Another time we had a helicopter in the
studio with Marc sitting in the cockpit."

Andy Williams, the legendary American balladeer and
master of the cool stage presence was in the studio at the
time and was completely stunned by events. He was
cajoled into sitting in the control room and then asked to
cue in Mr. Bolan.

"Andy couldn't believe it when he saw Marc, who was
sitting on the rotor blades whizzing round and round. We
had rotated the blades by using an electric motor. He said
all those things Americans like to say: 'Gee, we don't have
anything like this back home!' "

Another American guest at *Supersonic* was also
entranced by Bolan. He was Dennis Weaver, better known

as the cowboy cop McCloud, who was then enjoying a hit single. Marc of course decided he wanted to record McCloud.

"Marc wanted to do everything. Once Marc got an idea he displayed a tenacity that was enviable. It developed into a big thing and you couldn't prise them apart. Basically, he desperately wanted to succeed. He had that right from the beginning, when Marc and June slept in the van on Wimbledon Common."

Mansfield was fascinated by Marc's lifestyle, and felt great affection for him. "When Marc had his son Rolan, everything revolved around the child and Gloria. Yet his domestic life was very strange. He remained nomadic and nocturnal. Rolan was a very happy child, so the relationship was obviously working. He brought Rolan to the studio a couple of times."

At this time Mansfield owned The Gate House, a spacious abode in Wimbledon that had once belonged to Oliver Reed, and Mike decided to hold a fancy dress party there. Rod Stewart and Britt Ekland came and held court in the kitchen. Marc arrived with Gloria and he was dressed in red velvet and lace in a kind of 18th century get up. No less than five BBC producers arrived as clerics, and the head of light entertainment came as Sir Francis Drake.

"After a while Gloria went home, as Marc got rather the worse for wear," says Mike. "So he stayed the night, asleep in the sauna. There was a rather bizarre breakfast scene the following morning, with everybody still in their fancy dress costumes - or what was left of them."

Although Mike could help Marc with his TV show, there was little more he could do than offer a sympathetic hearing to Marc's wilder plans for the future. "He wanted to create a big pop opera, blending past, present and future. But he was like Lionel Bart. He would get a great idea and then do nothing about it for ages. Marc never reached what David Bowie had reached out to and touched. That glittering prize was just beyond his reach. Marc didn't ever achieve full international recognition - and I don't know why. I can't put my finger on why he wasn't accepted in America. In terms of image, maybe he was too soon for them. It was his greatest frustration that he wasn't accepted there."

At the last *Supersonic* it was decided to go back to the show's original format and do away with the effects. "We had tasted success and gone through blowing everything up. So for the last number I invited all the artists to join together and let them get on with it." The line up of talent included Marc Bolan, Elkie Brookes, Alvin Stardust, Ray Davies, Dave Edmunds, Steve Currie and Dino Dines from Marc's band. They decided to play 'Sweet Little Rock'n'Roller'. It was totally unrehearsed and they didn't know how to end it. Suddenly Marc vanished from the prancing troupe desperately trying to keep in time and tune. The door of Mike's control room opened and in walked Marc, insisting that the producer should come down and join in the chorus. Mike guessed what was up. "I knew what he wanted. He wanted to direct the show. But I couldn't relinquish the reins. I sent him down to the studio and he finished the number. And that was the last time we worked together. The waters of my mind may be muddy, but Marc stands out like a bright diamond in my memories."

Marc was immensely grateful for Mike's support and encouragement. One morning a large removal van arrived at his door and the struggling workmen heaved out a large Bel-Ami juke box. It was stocked full of Marc Bolan records.

In the summer of 1976 T. Rex released one of their best singles in a long time, 'I Love To Boogie'. It put Marc back into the Top Twenty, and gave his band something to sink their teeth into. He claimed he wrote the number in ten minutes.

He also released his last but one album, 'Futuristic Dragon', and hit the road, taking a dragon with him, and loyal fans cheered him to the echo. The music scene was just a few months away from the sudden outburst of punk rock, and Marc swiftly saw its potential. Far from being terrified by the arrival of the Sex Pistols, the Clash and the Damned, he loftily pronounced that it was a sort of 'electric skiffle' and that he had been its originator. In the middle of all this outburst of new youthful energy from a new wave of bands, he unleashed 'Laser Love', which proved to be a flop.

It was yet another setback that Marc had learned to take in his stride. His response was simply to form a new band and start playing more 'live' performances than ever. This new band was his most powerful and professional outside of a recording studio. It included the top bass player Herbie Flowers, now a key member of the highly successful Sky. Tony Newman, who had worked with David Bowie, was on drums, and he retained Dino Dines on keyboards. Miller Anderson came in on guitar to replace Jack Green, and both Steve Currie and Gloria left. But Marc continued to record Gloria, and they performed a duet on the old pop hit 'To Know Him Is To Love Him'. Early in 1977, the band rehearsed hard, and then T.Rex put out what was to be its last album, 'Dandy In The Underworld'.

It really seemed as if 1977 was going to be Marc's year. He wore smart new clothes, dyed his hair with a golden streak and went on tour with punk band the Damned, much to the astonishment of the rock establishment. Marc did an enormous amount to encourage the new bands and lived up to his latest title - The Godfather Of Punk. Said Rat Scabies, drummer with the Damned, after Marc's death: "He was one of our biggest inspirations, one of our few pop idols. He helped us a lot on tour, he looked after us, and he and his band gave us a lot of advice about our music. When he was at his peak, all today's punks were just waking up to music, and he was one of the biggest influences on them."

Many other musicians who worked with Marc during this period remember him with great fondness and had a high regard for his dedication. They felt a part of Bolan's dream machine. Herbie Flowers is moved by the fact that he still receives a stream of letters and 'phone calls from Bolan fans. And he's ready to talk to them at any time. "They just like to call me up to reminisce," says Herbie. He laughs wryly at the reasons why Marc asked him to work for T.Rex. "It was because I've got this stupid name. He wanted to work with a guy called Herbie Flowers! Then he asked me what drummer I wanted and of course it had to be Tony

Newman, because we had worked together on David Bowie's 'Diamond Dogs' L.P.

"I was with Marc for the last eighteen months of his life. I worked on all his last shows and sessions and I loved him. He was a real elfin space-cadet. There's only been four real pop stars in this country and Marc was one of them. The others were David Bowie, Gary Glitter and David Essex. To me, Marc had total star quality. But when we were on the road, Marc travelled in the coach with the rest of us. There was no special limo for Marc. We went to Europe, and did a couple of tours of Britain. We were all getting ready to go to America when the crash came."

Herbie was proud of the band, and he realised that although the public had once chucked Marc out, he had come back, like Cassius Clay, fighting. "The media really tried to put him down, and the more so when they saw the names of well known session musicians on the back of his LP. They were the same people who praised us when we played anonymously on albums by David or Lou Reed."

Herbie recorded many sessions with Marc at London's Air Studios, and recalls that Marc also sat in on many of his friends' albums. "They used to like having him around to ogle at him. He always got the stars out. David Bowie loved him, and he appeared on his TV show *Marc* at a time when he was turning every other offer down. We have a lot to thank Marc for, and yet he is always excluded from the big rock'n'roll history books and documentaries. Presley never wrote a song, and stars like him never got to meet the people. But there was Marc, living in Barnes, working away..."

Herbie's daughter, now aged twenty, used to go on tour with the band, and Marc would sit and chat to her for hours, reading poetry. Herbie tells how the rest of the band would send up their leader. Tony Newman, who had once been the drummer in Sounds Incorporated, and had been around the rock scene for years, liked to imitate the way Marc talked and the way he gave interviews as the big star. But Marc was impervious - and always laughed at the jokes. The mockery was affectionate, says Herbie: "There was a relationship between the musicians that the public and the press never got to hear about, because it's secret and precious."

Many were contemptuous of Marc's guitar playing, of his attempts to come on like Hendrix or Clapton. But Herbie, who has played with the finest musicians in the world, including the classical-turned-rock player John Williams, said: "Marc could play just one long note throughout a solo and it was really clever. Another guy could play 700 notes in a solo and it would mean nothing."

On the last T.Rex tour in 1977 the band played a lot of new material, as well as hits like 'Jeepster' and 'I Love To Boogie'. Bolan as band leader had all the right instincts to anticipate the mood of each audience, night after night.

"Sometimes he'd just play the intro, and we'd have to go straight into the number if he felt it was the right one to play for the audience. I just love to play bass - it stops me head aching - and I can only do it properly behind somebody like Marc. He was really a theatrical person. If he was around now he'd be writing plays and music for the theatre."

With a solid powerhouse band behind him, and the support of a new generation of admirers, Marc's future seemed brighter than it had for ages. June Bolan naturally followed events from afar, and sometimes found herself driving past his new house, drawn perhaps by the magnetism she still couldn't resist.

"He looked so together and happy, and I really felt things would be good for him." June was most impressed by his

new TV series *Marc* that was to prove, tragically, to be his last major achievement.

He recorded seven shows for Granada, and the last one was taped just a few days before his death. It almost seemed as if fate were gathering together all of Marc's friends for an unwitting farewell. Just before the last filming session, his publicist Keith Altham invited Marc's favourite journalists to come up to Manchester to watch Bolan and Bowie in action. There would be no interviews, but it would be a good chance to witness a unique event. Keith mentioned that he was worried about Bolan. His friends were reporting that Marc refused to eat, wouldn't drink and was almost wasting away.

When they got to Manchester the journalists spent much of the day being hustled out of the studio by David Bowie's bodyguard. But nobody wanted to pester Bowie anyway - all eyes were on Marc, who didn't have a bodyguard and invited everybody into his dressing room, hugged and kissed them, and was generally brimming over with high spirits. They were to be severely dampened, however, when things began to go wrong with the recording. But it turned out to be one of the funniest episodes in the careers of both stars. There were tears, outbursts of swearing, bitter rows and the breaking of light bulbs during the rehearsals and recording. The studio was the one normally used by the team that make *Coronation Street*.

Involved in all this were trade unionists, concerned with tea breaks and overtime, technicians anxious about camera angles and split-second timing, and rock people, ramshackle, untogether and temperamental.

Producer Muriel Young had to cope with the increasing fury of the other acts on the show, who had to wait around for hours while Marc and David tried to get their historic jamming routine together. Round and round the studio wandered the various musicians, with pressmen hiding behind them, trying to dodge Bowie's private and wholly unauthorised security man.

One band, Generation X, turned up three hours late, without any equipment, and Eddie & The Hot Rods waited around for two days without getting in front of the cameras. But Marc was in his element as a television star and part-time artistic director. One of the studio bosses cried out in despair when Marc began bellowing instructions: "I don't know why I'm the floor manager", he said. And Marc told him "When you've got your name up in lights, you've gotta take responsibilities."

Marc was putting on a performance that seemed like a cross between Judy Garland and Louis B. Mayer. But Barrie Masters, lead singer with the Hot Rods kept demanding: "Is he queer?". Then Marc sailed past him in the corridor calling out coyly: "What shall I wear? I know, the green dress with black suspenders." Eventually he turned up wearing up a kind of leopard-skin creation that would have given a leopard a nasty turn.

Marc's PR, Keith, had just recovered a few weeks previously from a heart attack, and it seemed likely that the afternoon would bring on another one. He was constantly verbally attacked by Barbara DeWitt, who was Bowie's American PR lady. She wanted to know what on earth Altham was doing by bringing so many journalists along in her artist's wake. In fact, the Bowie entourage was being very snooty, but David distanced himself from the whole affair and smiled coolly in all directions. He had come specially for the show, all the way from Switzerland, where he lived in a rarefied atmosphere. He had brought a lot of protection he didn't really need, and gradually he began to realise that rock'n'roll in England is only an

extension of the saloon bar, and not really such a big deal. At least Marc always appreciated that.

Marc once said: "All the so-called glamour of rock - riding about in airplanes and sitting in limousines - once you've done it once or twice - it's bloody boring. There is very little glamour in rock'n'roll. Hotel suites are very boring. All you really want to do is go home and put your feet up. That sounds very, gee whizz, doesn't it? I like to go home and sit with my parents or my kid Rolan, and relax with them. With fame, or so-called wealth, you get so much aggravation."

There was certainly plenty of aggravation in the studio on that afternoon. While Marc was putting on his stage gear in the tiny hot dressing-room reserved for him, the Heart Throbs dance-troupe performed a rather apt number called 'Ain't It Strange What Some People Will Do', dressed for the occasion in see-thru plastic bowler hats. There was some diversion while Bowie's ever zealous bodyguard tried to throw someone out of the studio. He was the local top official of the telly workers' union, who had the power to black-out most of the nation's screens by snapping his fingers. Once the bodyguard had been calmed down, work continued.

The Hot Rods had to mime to a backing track, and then Generation X arrived, late and breathless, in an aggressive mood. They had broken down on the M1 and had no equipment. Offers were made by T.Rex to lend them equipment and they discussed whether or not to smash up Marc's guitar. "What will it cost us — £400?"

The band had to play their number five times to get it right, and were constantly being stopped by the technicians. Marc repeated the same introduction. "This is Generation X. They had a new singer, Billy Idol who is supposed to be as pretty as me. I ain't so sure. Check it out." Eventually he stumbled over the words at the sixth repeat. "My brain weren't connected to me leg," he explained with a grin. Meanwhile, more rows were breaking out. Generation X's manager bellowed abuse across the studio floor at Producer Muriel, and as a ladylike professional she simply walked away. "It's appalling," the manager told the world. "Now they are only going to do half the song or pull it out. We'll do *Top Of The Pops* instead. Let's go!" He made a move for the exits, but the band stayed put.

Marc, like Muriel, seemed oblivious to this sort of behaviour. He really didn't want anything to spoil his big day, and he had seen this kind of temperamental behaviour all before; he had contributed some himself over the years. He sat in his dressing room for a while watching the previous week's show which was actually going out on the network while they were recording the next one. On the screen he was singing the old Chris Montez hit 'Let's Dance' with tremendous verve. He followed it up with his latest hit single, 'Celebrate Summer'. Muriel Young joined him for a while to keep away from the rampaging monsters of the New Wave. It was a temporary oasis of sanity. Years later, Muriel remembered that day when she last saw her old friend alive.

She met Marc when he was 15 and she was presenting the ITV children's show, *Five O'Clock Club*. She remembered Marc coming on the show together with Allen Warren, who she described as one of the 'helpers'. She was immediately struck by Bolan's looks. "Marc had a lovely face, and he was very cheeky and cool. I used to like him wearing his neatly cropped hair, and I hated his Afro! But he never went back to the old smart style. He often came on *Five O'Clock Club*, and he always had a great aura about

him even then. He was so small and handsome and very funny."

After spells as a quiz show presenter for Southern TV, where she met Mike Mansfield and Marc once more, she worked as a disc jockey for Radio Luxembourg, presenting the EMI show. She became a TV producer, and an early success was the Bay City Rollers' 'Shang A Lang', followed by 'Breakers' which featured new groups. Then she began to look around for another artist who would be a suitable peg for a series.

"I was having lunch in Rags restaurant in London with Mike Mansfield, when in walked Marc. I was actually discussing with Mike what sort of group I should feature. I didn't mention my idea to him right away, as I thought he would be too grand to do a kids' show. But I rang him up and he was absolutely delighted with the idea."

"There were seven shows altogether, and Marc was a great help to me in spotting new bands to put on. I was right off punk rock myself, and didn't like their attitudes. Marc said: "Don't be daft - it's going to happen". I checked all the lyrics of their songs first. I wasn't going to have any 'kicking Granny in the crutch' stuff, because I had my responsibilities presenting a show for children. But Marc found the bands and we put the Jam on TV for the first time and Generation X. A lot of groups got their first television appearances on Marc's shows. And that was all due to Marc's guidance, not me. He *told* me what to present, and it was very exciting, when you look back.

"Marc had his own band T.Rex on the show, and they were all very nice. The musicians used to call themselves grandads because they were much older than Marc. He did four numbers and then we'd feature the guests. On the show Marc was very high camp and cheeky, and sent everybody up rotten. We had a press reception and I'd be ready with my speech and then Marc would say the most terrible things, and I'd faint with horror. He'd say to me afterwards: ' "Never mind darling, it makes a good story".'

Everybody wanted to be on Marc's show and one of the most important bands who got their first TV break were the Boomtown Rats. Marc told Muriel that although punk rock wasn't particularly clever music, it would be enormous for three years and then sort itself out, with the good artists becoming part of the establishment and the rest dropping by the wayside. "Which was exactly what happened, of course," says Muriel.

Back at the studio on that September afternoon the floor was cleared for Marc and David to rehearse their big number. They were joined by Herbie Flowers, Dino Dines and Tony Newman. To the uninitiated it all sounded like a bit of a shambles. In fact, the song was only just put together in time and remained untitled, a bit of casual rock jamming, but as they got into their stride the music began to sound very funky, with Marc blazing away enthusiastically on his guitar.

The relationship between Bowie and Bolan dated back many years, from a time when Marc had achieved stardom well before the Beckenham whizzkid. Bowie, himself a bit of a Mod in the Sixties, had always looked up to Bolan, and used to go round to his London flat and sit on the floor and discuss music. Marc gave him words of encouragement, and also recommended that he split away from his manager and find a new one. He was joined in this campaign by Tony Visconti, and of course Bowie followed their advice. He later emerged, wearing a dress for the cover of his Visconti produced album, 'The Man Who Sold The World', which launched him into the Seventies to become an even bigger star than Bolan.

They had first recorded together in February 1970 when David brought an ad hoc group together called Hype. This included Marc on guitar, Mike Woodmansey (drums), Mick Ronson (guitar) and Tony Visconti (bass). Rick Wakeman also played some piano on the session which produced a rare single version of 'The Prettiest Star'. David lost the master tape of this performance and he later rerecorded the song for his 'Alladin Sane' album in 1973 with Mick Ronson playing the guitar parts previously played by Bolan.

It was a shame the pair did not work together more often, because there was undoubtedly a magic to the atmosphere in the studio that transcended all the upsets and arguments. David stood tall and detached beside Marc, as if he were floating in another space time and dimension, while Marc bounced energetically at his feet, the court jester momentarily in awe of his royal patron.

The Sixties and all their memories must have swept over Marc, because he suddenly burst into a chorus of 'Debora' harking back to his days with Tyrannosaurus Rex. It turned out to be a new version, but unfortunately the backing track slipped out of synchronization. "I don't mind lip-synching, but when it's the WRONG verse..." complained Marc tartly.

David gazed steadily into the middle distance. Then came a bellowed announcement. "Will anybody not on the show please leave the studio!"

"Oh, why did we come?" wailed the Hot Rods, as they too were hustled away.

David readied himself for his big solo number, which turned out to be 'Heroes'. He rolled up the trouser legs of his jeans to reveal laced boots and stood cooly in front of the microphone, waiting for the studio chatter to stop.

Ignoring some feedback he began to sing, slowly and with a surprisingly deep voice. After a pregnant pause he suddenly bellowed: "I will be king and you will be queen ... we can be heroes just for one day!" Talk about upstaging the opposition. It looked like he had been waiting all day just to sing that line.

Now it was time for Marc to rejoin David and attempt to take their hastily sketched out number. David had his face made up and Marc anxiously called to the floor manager: "Do you want me front or back?"

"Just touch your toes Marc," shouted one of the Hot Rods still waiting on the opposite rostrum to do their number. The mighty duo began their number, and Billy Idol said approvingly from the sidelines: "It's got that disco beat all right."

"What an old poofter," grumbled a roadie uncharitably.

Suddenly there was a commotion on stage and the number ground to a halt. "We're getting electric shocks up here," shrieked Marc, pointing towards the microphones. Nobody moved. Time was ticking dangerously away. At 7pm the union would pull the plugs out - prompt.

Attempts were made by the production team to stop the band from making more noise. "We're rehearsing, actually," said Marc, somewhat put out. David stood quietly on one side, smiling and unperturbed. But suddenly he frowned. "That wasn't the actual take was it?" he asked, as the truth began to dawn. "What do you mean not really?" he stormed at the technician who caught his icy blast. "Either it was or it wasn't." And to everybody's astonishment David shouted "1, 2, 3, 4!" Tony Newman uncertainly set the drums rolling once more and at this point Marc fell off the stage with excitement.

"A wooden box for Marc to stand on please," said David. "Look, we've got to do that again, it wasn't finished." But

the studio man was calling, "Let's have the Rods please."
The Rods obediently scrambled onto their rostrum to start
recording, and in retaliation David and Marc instantly
started jamming.

At 7pm precisely all the lights went out and the
technicians disappeared, heading for home and a nice
cup of cocoa. "You've got a black-out mate," called a voice
from the floor. A furious row broke out between the Rods
and the producer when it was realized there was no time
left for them to do their number.

"This is really unfair," said their singer, Barrie Masters.
"We've been waiting here all day to go on and we came up
from London yesterday. That's two days wasted." The Rods
stormed off to their dressing room where a lot of swearing
went on. Bolan locked himself in his dressing room in tears.
But David called him up to the viewing room to watch the
results of the day's work on video. Marc wiped away his tears
and joined in the laughter when he saw how they looked.
When Marc fell off the stage David hooted. "Oh that's really
Polaroid! You've gotta keep that ending!" Even the
bodyguard smiled.

David travelled on the train, having left Marc in
Manchester to help salvage the video tape and turn it into a
show. At first Bowie hid himself in a locked compartment
with all the blinds drawn, but when he discovered the Hot
Rods were in the next carriage he came out to share beer
and chicken legs with them. He relaxed and pronounced
that the show had been "a lot of fun". He explained that he
also recorded another special guest appearance on a TV
show, and much to everybody's surprise revealed that he
had sung a duet with none other than Bing Crosby.

There was a bizarre footnote to all this. For not only was
Marc to die before the show he recorded with David was
screened, but Bing Crosby also died a month after his show
with David and before it was televised that Christmas. Bowie
had returned to Europe when he heard the news of Marc's
death, and he flew back for the funeral.

Muriel Young had also wished Marc farewell at the studio.
"We had a dreadful day because of the time factor. The
union wanted an extra week's pay for the extra time. They
turned down the overtime because they couldn't get treble.
But two days were booked which I thought would be enough.
David Bowie had flown in especially for the show because
he loved Marc and wanted to do it for him. While we were
going through their number Marc fell off the stage and
broke his guitar. That's really what started to give him
electric shocks. We couldn't get the guitar mended in time,
and when we tried to borrow a guitar from another band we
found they had all gone home.

"We were running out of time and in the end we had a
minute and a half of jam session left of Bowie and Marc
together. They couldn't believe that the technicians would
pull the plugs. But the boys will do that, even if you are the
Queen of England. That's why all the lights went out. David
took it in his stride, but Marc was desperately upset."

Marc and Muriel got together the following week to work
once more on the show, and insert the captions.

"That was the last time I saw Marc. Two days later, on the
Friday morning, he was dead. I never spoke to him again
after that night in the studio. You wouldn't believe the letters
of hatred and abuse I got for cutting them off after one
minute 30 seconds. They said: "You didn't need Generation
X, you should have given the time to this wonderful
partnership." I wrote back to say it wasn't my fault. It should
have lasted five minutes, but we had to run the captions.
The last shot was of David laughing as Marc fell off the
stage."

People were waking up, getting out of bed, scurrying to work, when the news came through that Marc Bolan was dead.

Some switched on their radios and heard a succession of old T. Rex hits. There had to be a reason for such an unexpected tribute.

Marc died when the purple Mini driven by Gloria Jones skidded off the road and crashed into a tree on Barnes Common. The car was travelling at between 40 and 50mph. The impact flattened the engine compartment, snapped off the gear lever and forced the steering wheel into the roof. Marc had taken the full force of the crash. He had been sitting in the front passenger seat, and his body was forced into the back of the car. His death had come just four weeks after the death, in America, of Elvis Presley.

B.P. Fallon was one of the many shocked by the news. Just a few weeks before he had been talking to Marc about the death of Elvis. Said Marc: "You know something, I'm glad I didn't get killed today. I wouldn't have got on the front covers." Maria Callas, the opera singer, had died the same day as Elvis, and of course he got all the coverage.

The crash happened just before 5am on Friday, 16 September 1977. The car had been travelling down a narrow road lined with trees towards the junction of Roehampton Lane with Upper Richmond Road. After the crash Gloria was taken to Queen Mary's Hospital, Roehampton, with serious facial injuries, and a broken jaw. She was not told the news of Marc's death for some time after the accident, until she showed sufficient signs of recovery. Richard Jones, Gloria's brother, had been following the Mini in another car. When he drove over a hump back bridge he found the smoking, steaming wreckage. Twenty yards of fencing had been torn down and the bark was stripped from the horse-chestnut tree which the Mini had struck. Later, fans were to turn the tree into a kind of shrine for Marc, and gathered there on the anniversary of his death.

June Bolan remembers waking early and vaguely hearing the phrase 'Bolan dies in car crash' on the radio, as she sat up in bed. She next received a call from Ronnie Money, the wife of bandleader Zoot Money. She told June the full story.

June rushed to Marc's parents' house, where there was a dreadul scene.

Marc's father slammed the door in her face. When Marc's brother Harry came out, apparently to comfort her, Mrs. Feld yelled abuse from the window and told her son: "Don't cuddle her. Kill her." They undoubtedly blamed June for having left Marc. Despite the ill-feeling, she went to the funeral, against the family's wishes. She kept herself out of sight, but managed to view the body, and found that Marc's face had been barely marked by the accident.

The funeral was held at Golders Green Crematorium on the following Tuesday, 20 September, and a party of mourners gathered at Marc's record company, EMI, in Manchester Square. Marc's old friend and producer Tony Visconti described the funeral as being "like a circus", but to most it seemed a sober and respectful gathering.

A procession of cars set off for Golders Green and as they turned into the grounds of the crematorium, groups of fans could be seen waiting. A few asked for autographs, but there was no unseemly jostling or noise, and most of the mourners were able to find themselves seats inside the packed chapel. David Bowie and Rod Stewart were among them.

Marc's mother sobbed aloud during the address by Rabbi Henry Goldstein when he said that there had been two Marc Bolans, one a loving son and the other an image projected on stage. Those who knew him in either role were united in their mourning.

Outside in the sunshine the mourners wiped away tears, and stood in respectful silence to inspect the floral tributes. The centre piece was a huge white swan made from chrysanthemums, four feet high with 'Marc' picked out in more flowers at the base.

Alvin Stardust, Steve Harley, Mary Hopkin, Linda Lewis, and members of the Damned and Brotherhood of Man were among those who paid their respects to Marc's memory, and there were more wreaths from Elton John, Cliff Richard, Keith Moon, Gary Glitter and of course, T. Rex. June later went to view the ashes, despite more opposition, and laid before the urn a bunch of gardenias. "They were Marc's favourite flowers, and only I knew that," she said.

After the funeral it was announced that David Bowie would set up a trust for Marc and Gloria's son, which would benefit him when he reached 18. And in Marc's will, which he had drawn up in 1973 he left equal amounts of £10,000 to both June and Gloria. The rest of his fortune went to family and friends.

At the inquest Gloria had to give evidence, and as her jaw was wired up she had to write down answers to the questions. A verdict of accidental death was returned.

Gloria and Richard Jones returned to America and later took Roland, then aged two, back to the States, away from Marc's parents, who had been looking after him.

There were more tragedies in the wake of Marc's death. Steve Peregrine Took died in 1980, and Steve Currie was killed in a road accident in Spain in 1981.

On the evening of Marc's death he had been to Morton's restaurant in Berkeley Square with Eric Hall, Richard and Gloria. Earlier Mike Mansfield had dropped by, and he remembers that Marc had asked him to direct a new series of TV shows he was planning. "He was wearing a red jester's jump suit. That epitomized Marc. He was a jester who laughed at us all and knew exactly what he was doing. I never went back to Morton's again after Marc's death."

There is a certain fatalism and cynicism about death and its contribution to the drama of rock music. There is a morbid curiosity about the passing of such stars as Jim

Morrison, Jimi Hendrix, or Buddy Holly. But in each case the reality of bereavement touches those who are closest and most understand the victim. In Marc's case there was a wider and more deepfelt sense of loss, because he had never been remote or distant. He had always maintained the closest contact with his fans and friends. It was true that he could take away the affection he gave so readily to people, often with an abruptness that hurt. But there was no malice in him, and as Eric Hall once said: "Everybody who knew him, loved him."

Said another friend, "He was very affectionate to people and he had warmth towards them. He made people feel excited and glad to be alive. He was very intimate with all the people he knew, and he didn't have any acquaintances — he only had close friends."

Of course, his friends recognized the ambition that drove him and greatly admired the self-confidence that so many lack which Marc had in abundance. Says B.P. Fallon with affection: "He was a very determined young chappie. It was just a matter of getting his spells right and he knew things would work."

Keith Altham, his publicist, who had known him for 14 years said: "I knew Marc first when I was a writer and then as a publicist and friend. It was a double tragedy that he died when he did, because he was coming back to the top again. His physical and mental health were better than they had been for some time, and he was ready to make the same impact on the scene that he did before. The New Wave had inspired him, and given him new enthusiasm."

Muriel Young, who had produced his last TV shows also paid tribute and described his death as a tragic loss: "Apart from being such a great professional who won the admiration of everyone in the studios, Marc had endeared himself to the whole team with his sense of mischief and fun, and most of all because he truly cared about his show, his fans, his colleagues and his music."

For Marc's contemporaries, those who grew up with him, the events that span ten or more years of triumph and excitement still seem remarkably fresh and recent. They still can't quite believe that Marc Bolan has gone. Nor his voice, his laughter or his hits.

Marc was a great kidder, but he never joked about his music, and you can hear his passionate intensity through all the songs he recorded over the years, the good ones and the bad ones. It was apparent on one of his earliest recordings, 'Desdemona' recorded with John's Children in 1967. On it, Marc took the unaccustomed role of backing singer on his own composition. He echoes Andy Ellison's lead vocals with proprietorial zeal, bringing life to the lyrics that his partner could not achieve, even with the best of intentions. The performance highlights how Marc had developed and refined his vocal style at a very early stage.

The more one listens to Marc, the more one realizes his greatest influence was himself. Could Chuck Berry have produced performances like 'Ride A White Swan', 'Hot Love' or 'Woodland Bop'? It seems highly unlikely.

Marc may have written his songs with a flurry of spontaneous combustion, much the same way he played guitar, but by writing his lyrics only minutes before a recording was due to start, he converted them into gold dust by the alchemy of the performance rather than by the wizardry of technology.

We should not be deceived. Marc Bolan was a professional. And even when his more grandiose claims were occasionally outweighed by his shortcomings, he was essentially an artist of the greatest integrity.

Chris Welch, August 2nd 1981.

UK DISCOGRAPHY

This UK discography is taken from the official world Marc Bolan discography compiled by John & Shan Bramley for Omnibus Press.

SINGLES

MARC BOLAN SOLO SINGLES

November 19, 1965.	The Wizard/Beyond The Rising Sun	Decca
June 3, 1966.	The Third Degree/San Francisco Poet	Decca
March, 1966.	Hippy Gumbo/Misfit	Parlophone

MARC BOLAN WITH JOHN'S CHILDREN

May 24, 1967.	Desdemona/Remember Thomas A Beckett	Track

Midsummer Night's Scene was never available in shops, band members sold them in clubs.

July 14, 1967.	Come And Play With Me In The Garden/Sara Crazy Child	Track
December, 1967.	Go Go Girl/Jagged Time Lapse	Track

MARC BOLAN WITH TYRANNOSAURUS REX

April 19, 1968.	Debora/Child Star	Regal Zonophone
August 23, 1968.	One Inch Rock/Salamanda Palaganda	Regal Zonophone
January 14, 1969.	Pewter Suiter/Warlord Of The Royal Crocodiles	Zonophone
July 25, 1969.	King Of The Rumbling Spires/Do You Remember	Zonophone
January 20, 1970.	By The Light Of A Magical Moon/Find A Little Wood	Zonophone

MARC BOLAN WITH DIB COCHRAN & THE EARWIGS

August, 1970.	Oh Baby/Universal Love	Bell

MARC BOLAN WITH T. REX

October 3, 1970.	Ride A White Swan/Is It Love/Summertime Blues	Fly
February 19, 1971.	Hot Love/Woodland Rock/The King Of The Mountain Cometh	Fly
July 2, 1971.	Get It On/There Was A Time/Raw Ramp	Fly
November 1, 1971.	Jeepster/Life's A Gas	Fly
January 21, 1972.	Telegram Sam/Cadilac/Baby Strange	T. Rex/EMI
March 24, 1972.	Debora/One Inch Rock/Woodland Bop/The Seal Of Seasons	Fly
May 5, 1972.	Metal Guru/Thunderwing/Lady	T. Rex/EMI
September 8, 1972.	Children Of The Revolution/Jitterbug Love/Sunken Rags	T. Rex/EMI
December 1, 1972.	Solid Gold Easy Action/Born To Boogie	T. Rex/EMI
March 2, 1973.	20th Century Boy/Free Angel	T. Rex/EMI
June 1, 1973.	The Groover/Midnight	T. Rex/EMI

MARC BOLAN WITH BIG CARROT

August, 1973.	Blackjack/Squint Eyed Mangle	EMI

ARC BOLAN WITH T. REX

vember 16, 1973.	Truck on (Tyke)/Sitting Here	T. Rex/EMI
bruary 9, 1974.	Teenage Dreams/Satisfaction Pony	T. Rex/EMI
y 13, 1974.	Light Of Love/Explosive Mouth	T. Rex/EMI

ARC BOLAN SOLO SINGLE

eased sometime in 1974. Jasper C. Debussy/Hippy Gumbo/The Perfumed Garden Of Gulliver Smith. Very early songs
m days with Track Records.

ARC BOLAN WITH T. REX

vember 1, 1974.	Zip Gun Boogie/Space Boss	T. Rex/EMI
ne 21, 1975.	New York City/Chrome Sitar	T. Rex/EMI

LEASED UNDER NAME OF T. REX DISCO PARTY

ptember 26, 1975.	Dreamy Lady/Do You Wanna Dance/Dock Of The Bay	T. Rex/EMI

MARC BOLAN WITH T. REX

Marc's Xmas Box should have been released Xmas 1975, but never reached shops, tracks were Christmas Bop/Metal Guru/Telegram Sam (T. Rex/EMI)

February 21, 1976.	London Boys/Solid Baby	T. Rex/EMI
April 6, 1976.	Hot Love/Get It On (re-issue)	Cube Records
June 5, 1976.	I Love To Boogie/Baby Boomerang	T. Rex/EMI
September 17, 1976.	Laser Love/Life's An Elevator	T. Rex/EMI

MARC BOLAN WITH GLORIA JONES

| January 14, 1977. | To Know Him Is To Love Him/City Port | EMI |

MARC BOLAN WITH T. REX

March 12, 1977.	The Soul Of My Suit/All Alone	T. Rex/EMI
May 30, 1977.	Dandy In The Underworld/Groove A Little/Tame My Tiger	T. Rex/EMI
August 5, 1977.	Celebrate Summer/Ride My Wheels	T. Rex/EMI
August 5, 1977.	Bolans Best + One	Cube Records
March 10, 1978.	Hot Love/Raw Ramp/Lean Woman Blues	Cube Records
April 11, 1978.	Crimson Moon/Jason B. Sad	T. Rex/EMI
September 27, 1979.	Life's A Gas/Find A Little Wood/Once Upon The Seas of Abyssinia/Blessed Wild Apple Girl	Cube Records
March 27, 1981.	Sing Me A Song/Endless Sleep/The Lilac Hand	Rarn Records
August, 1981.	Jeepster/Get It On	Cube/Dakota
September 11, 1981.	You Scare Me To Death/The Perfumed Garden of Gulliver Smith	Cherry Red
February 5, 1982.	Mellow Love/Foxy Boy/Lunacy's Back	Marc On Wax
February 12, 1982.	Mellow Love/Foxy Boy/Lunacy's Back/Rock Me	Marc On Wax
April, 1982.	Telegram Sam/Cadilac/Baby Strange	T. Rex/EMI
May, 1982.	The Wizard/Beyond The Rising Sun/Rings Of Fortune	Cherry Red
June, 1982.	Life's A Gas/Find A Little Wood/Once Upon The Seas Of Abyssinia/Blessed Wild Apple Girl	Marc On Wax
August, 1982.	Deep Summer/Oh Baby/One Inch Rock	Marc On Wax

ALBUMS

TYRANNOSAURUS REX

July, 1968.	My People Were Fair & Had Sky In Their Hair	Regal Zonophone
October, 1968.	Prophets, Seers And Sages	Regal Zonophone
May, 1969.	Unicorn	Regal Zonophone
March, 1970.	Beard Of Stars	Regal Zonophone

T. REX

December, 1970.	T. Rex	Fly
March, 1971.	Best Of T. Rex	Fly
September, 1971.	Electric Warrior	Fly
Spring, 1972.	My People/Prophets Seers & Sages (Double)	Fly
May, 1972.	Bolan Boogie	Fly
Summer, 1972.	Unicorn/Beard Of Stars (double-reissue)	Fly
June, 1972.	Hard On Love (Very rare as album stopped)	Track
July, 1972.	The Slider	T. Rex/EMI
March, 1973.	Tanx	T. Rex/EMI
Autumn, 1973.	Great Hits	T. Rex/EMI
Febr ary, 1974.	Zinc Alloy & The Hidden Riders Of Tomorrow	T. Rex/EMI
June, 1974.	A Beginning Of Doves	Track
February, 1975.	Bolan's Zip Gun	T. Rex/EMI
February, 1976.	Futuristic Dragon	T. Rex/EMI
March, 1977.	Dandy In The Underworld	T. Rex/EMI
1978.	Marc The Words & Music 1947-1977	Cube Records
1979.	Solid Gold T. Rex	EMI
1980.	Unobtainable T. Rex	EMI
August, 1981.	T. Rex In Concert	Marc Records
October, 1981.	You Scare Me To Death	Cherry Red
February, 1982.	Across The Airwaves	Cube/Dakota
June, 1982.	The Children Of Rarn Suite (10")	Marc On Wax
August, 1982.	Billy Super Duper	Marc On Wax